THE *Glory* OF EASTER

THE *Glory* OF EASTER

MELINDA RATHJEN

EDITOR

Guideposts

Published by Ideals Publications
A Guideposts Company
Nashville, Tennessee
www.idealsbooks.com

Color separations by Precision Color Graphics, Franklin, Wisconsin
Printed and bound in the U.S.A.

Publisher, Peggy Schaefer
Editor, Melinda Rathjen
Permissions Editor, Patsy Jay

Designed by Eve DeGrie

10 9 8 7 6 5 4 3 2 1

ADDITIONAL PHOTOGRAPHY AND ART CREDITS:

Cover, Mount Rainier National Park, Washington. Photograph © Tomas Kaspar

Page 2, photograph © Lisa Hubbard/Botanica/Jupiter Images; page 3, photograph © Mark Turner/Botanica/Jupiter Images; pages
5 and 12, photograph © Igor Dvoretskiy/iStockphoto; pages 5 and 62, photograph © Sascha Burkard/iStockphoto; pages 5 and 90,
photograph © Ryan KC Wong/iStockphoto; pages 5 and 122, photograph © cloki/iStockphoto; pages 5 and 144, photograph ©
Lilyana Vinogradova /iStockphoto; pages 6–7, Red House Lake in Allegany State Park, New York. Photograph © Carr Clifton;
pages 32–33, Lost Lake and Mount Hood, Oregon. Photograph © Dennis Frates; pages 66–67, photograph © Tim Hurst/Roam
Images/Jupiter Images; pages 102–103, Mission San Xavier del Bac chapel, Arizona. Photograph © Dennis Frates; pages 134–135,
pond in Black Rock Desert National Conservation Area, Nevada. Photograph © Dennis Frates; background pattern used throughout © Bill Noll/iStockphoto; various decorative elements throughout use vector illustrations © John Woodcock/iStockphoto.

ACKNOWLEDGMENTS

BARKMAN, ALMA. "A Different Celebration" from *Daily Guideposts*, April 2002. Used by permission, all rights reserved. BONELL,
HAROLD C. "The Door" from *Prayers of Those Who Knew Him Best*. Dorrance Publishing Company, Inc., 1967. CHAFIN, KENNETH.
"I Was There" from *Daily Guideposts*, April 2001. Used by permission, all rights reserved. CROWELL, GRACE NOLL. "Light the
Candles." Originally entitled "Easter" from *Let the Sun Shine In*. Copyright © 1970. Used by permission of Revell, a division of Baker
Publishing Group. "Christ Is Risen."by Grace Noll Crowell. Previously published in *Ideals Easter*, 1965, by permission of the author
and used here by permission of Claire Cumberworth. DUNCAN, KEN. "Crowds and Conflicts," "Triumph and Tension," and
"Unending Journey" from *Where Jesus Walked* by Ken Duncan. Copyright © 2006 by the author. Used by permission of Integrity
Publishers: Thomas Nelson Inc. GRAHAM, BILLY. "On the Third Day" from *Unto the Hills* by Billy Graham. Copyright © 1996 by
the author. Used by permission, all rights reserved. GUTHRIE, NANCY. "The Cross Shows Me the Joy of Jesus" and "Reconciliation"
from *The One Year Book of Hope* by Nancy Guthrie. Copyright © 2005 by the author. Published by Tyndale House Publishers.
MARSHALL, PETER. "The Upper Room," originally "The Last Supper," and "Lovest Thou Me?" from *The First Easter*. Used by per-
mission of Peter Marshall, Peter Marshall Ministries. MAUS, CYNTHIA PEARL. "That Resurrection Morn" from *Christ and the Fine
Arts*. Copyright © 1938 by editor/author Cynthia Pearl Maus. Published by Harper & Bros. OLSON, ENID MARTELL. "Grace
Incarnate" from *Poems of Faith for the Christian Year* by Enid Martell Olson, © 1959 by Augsburg Publishing House. Used by permis-
sion of the publisher. OUR THANKS TO THE FOLLOWING AUTHORS OR THEIR HEIRS, some of whom we have been unable to locate:
Georgia B. Adams, Christal Ahlemann, Beverly J. Anderson, June Masters Bacher, Esther York Burkholder, Dolores Cains, Lansing
Christman, Josephine Rice Creelman, Alberta Dodson, Ella E. Doxsee, Donita M. Dyer, Jessie Cannon Eldridge, Abigail Falk, M.
Mae Fisher, Inez Franck, Merle Marquis Frank, Loise Pinkerton Fritz, Mona K. Guldswog, Isaac Massey Haldeman, Mary Imogene
Harris, Edith Helstern, Kay Hoffman, Reginald Holmes, Pamela Kennedy, Brian R. King, Cleo King, Caroline S. Kotowicz,
Raymond Kresensky, Kathleen Lemmon, John Richard Moreland, Letitia Morse Nash, Raymond Orner, Hattie Pope, Alice
Kennelly Roberts, Alta Robinson, Elma Rowbotham, Gertrude Rudberg, Alice M. Stewart, Evelyn Weeks Taylor, Mable Clare
Thomas, Grace V. Watkins, Helen Welshimer, Laurie E. Dawson Wilcox, Kathryn Stephenson Wilhelm, Carice Williams, Helen
Williams, William Arnette Wofford.

Unless otherwise noted, all Scripture quotations are taken from the *Holy Bible*, King James Version.

Scripture quotations marked NLT are taken from the *Holy Bible*, New Living Translation, copyright © 1996. Used by permission of Tyndale House Publishers, Inc., Carol Stream, Illinois 60188. All rights reserved.

Scripture quotations marked NIV are taken from the *Holy Bible*, New International Version®. NIV®. Copyright © 1973, 1978,
1984 by International Bible Society. Used by permission of Zondervan. All rights reserved.

Every effort has been made to establish ownership and use of each selection in this book. If contacted, the publisher will be
pleased to rectify any inadvertent errors or omissions in subsequent editions.

TABLE OF CONTENTS

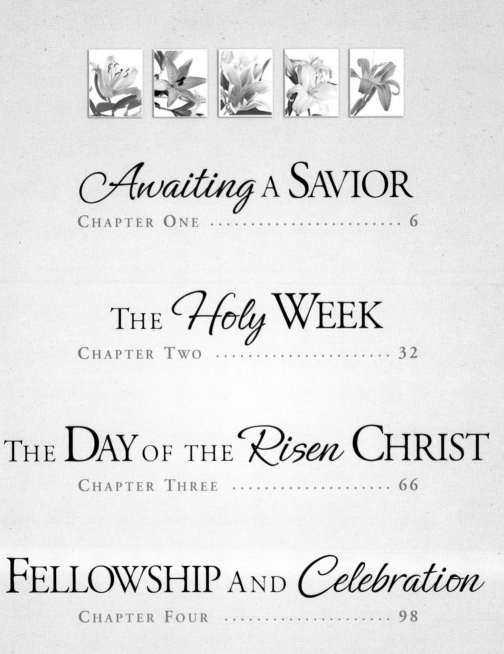

Awaiting a Savior

CHAPTER ONE

WHAT EASTER MEANS

ALTA ROBINSON

At last, the long, cold days of winter are over, and spring is here again. With spring comes Easter, the most beautiful season of all the year. Spring and Easter are synonymous; together they bring new life to the world and new hope to the hearts of people.

The name *Easter* comes from a very old Anglo-Saxon word that means "goddess of spring and light," in whose honor spring festivals were held long ago. The symbolism of these early festivals has blended with our meaning of Easter, and we now celebrate spring and Easter together. The purity of a white spring lily has become our symbol of resurrection, and the rabbit and the Easter egg the symbols of new life. Even the Easter bonnets and the bright new dresses of spring are the unconscious expression of people trying to match the colors of nature.

Spring is a time of rejoicing. A whirring of new sounds is in the air, as well as a stirring of unseen forces, like the breath of God re-creating life in the world. The miracle is already happening in the maple tree outside the window; the buds are swelling, and soon the tiny shoots will appear and unfold into the tender green leaves. The same thing is happening across the far reaches of the lawn as the green blades of grass slowly push themselves through the dead grass of the year before.

We like to hear the music and sounds of spring after the deep silences of the long winter days. At first we strain our ears to catch the note of a single bird, and then, almost before we know it, the whole air is filled with a dozen birds' glad new song. With our windows open, we can hear the wild Canadian geese on the neighbor's pond as they proudly honk their mating calls. At night we like to listen to the hum and stitch of innumerable voices in the insect world, some so faint that the human ear can hardly detect them. The best sound of all is the laughter of playing children, whose signs of spring are their own: a baseball bat and a fishing pole, a hopscotch ring and bulging pockets of agate marbles. We like to see their kites high in the sky, bravely tacking against a steady wind and trailing a long string in the air.

Spring and Easter are a time of hope, when we yearn to put into action the

Bluebells in Washington Park Arboretum, Seattle, Washington. Photograph © Mary Liz Austin/Austin Donnelly Photography

dreams and plans of our leisure days. The farmer, no matter how meager his harvest of the year before, again tills and plants his soil with eager expectancy.

Easter is the symbol of man's highest hopes, the promise of life after death. This hope is fulfilled in the Resurrection of Jesus from the dead, which is the basis of the true meaning of Easter.

Yes, spring and Easter are here again, bringing their meaning of life and hope. And in this hope we will rejoice and be glad.

Easter Outlook

INEZ FRANCK

I view the earth adorned in snowflake plum,
The bluebells ringing down the garden rows,
And everywhere is live with robin song,
The verdant country fields that spring bestows.
The little streams come by with woodland glee;
The hyacinths are dancing in the sun.
The world awakes to miracles of love
And tells a message clear for everyone.

I think this loveliness unfolds a plan.
It is God's way of speaking to my heart
And showing life with great expectancy—
The living hope that Easter scenes impart.
The Resurrection glory fills these hours
With songs of joy that only He can give;
I look to Easter's everlasting light
And feel because He lives, I too shall live.

10

*Spring is a birth
time for the world—
a resurrection
of new hope.*

—AGNES DAVENPORT BOND

*Soybean field in Champaign County, Illinois. Photograph
© Jason Lindsey/Perceptive Visions Stock Photography*

THE WORLD AWAITS EASTER

12

For, lo, the winter is past, the rain is over and gone; The flowers appear on the earth; the time of the singing of birds is come, and the voice of the turtle is heard in our land; The fig tree putteth forth her green figs, and the vines with the tender grape give a good smell.
—SONG OF SOLOMON 2:11–13

Thus we come to Easter . . . celebrating life and hope and the ultimate substance of belief— reaching, like the leaf itself, for something beyond, ever beyond.
—HAL BORLAND

Fair lilies with their crystal light
And eager, joyous greetings bright
Proclaim the Lord has risen again
And put asunder death and pain!
—JOSEPHINE RICE CREELMAN

Our Lord has written
the promise of the Resurrection
not in books alone,
but in every leaf in springtime.
—MARTIN LUTHER

Not from the borrowed tomb alone
Was Christ raised up on high,
For in each flower He comes forth,
Loving the Easter sky.
—WILLIAM WALTER DE BOLT

This newness, this freshness is all around:
This beauty is bursting forth from the ground;
The singing of birds flying by on wing,
The pure air of early spring—
Symbols of a new life, of one reborn
With spirit of Easter morn.

—MARY IMOGENE HARRIS

See the land, her Easter keeping,
Rises as her Maker rose.
Seeds, so long in darkness sleeping,
Burst at last from winter snows.
Earth with heaven above rejoices.

—CHARLES KINGSLEY

The good intent of God became the Christ

And lived on earth—the living love of God—

That men might draw to closer touch with heaven,

Since Christ in all the ways of man hath trod.

—JOHN OXENHAM

Springtime . . . invites you
to try out its splendor . . .
to believe anew, to realize that
the same Lord who renews the trees
and buds and blossoms is ready to
renew your life with hope and courage.

—CHARLES R. SWINDOLL

The world itself keeps Easter Day,
And Easter larks are singing;
And Easter flow'rs are blooming gay,
And Easter buds are springing.
    Alleluia! Alleluia!
The Lord of all things lives anew,
And all His works are living too.
    Alleluia! Alleluia!

—JOHN MASON NEALE

Spring . . . it is a natural resurrection,
an experience of immortality.

—HENRY DAVID THOREAU

EASTER AND SPRING

LANSING CHRISTMAN

Easter and spring come almost hand in hand, offering an appropriate ritual for both the observance of the Resurrection and the arrival of spring. The risen Christ brought great joy to His people on the day of His Resurrection. And spring, a new season of birth, of hope and faith, brings joy to mankind.

Year after year, each season in turn assumes its role in the calendar of time. Spring, with its songs and flutes, buds and blossoms, brings cheer and strength and hope and the solace of faith.

That first spring blossom is as glorious to the eye as is the meaning of the Resurrection to the heart and soul of man. Humanity cannot ignore the greatness of all things in nature and life and cannot ignore that behind the great changes in the seasons and behind all life is the work, labor, and love of the Master of all.

One cannot close his eyes to the spring beauty that unfolds around him: the new green, the flowers, the longer days of sun, the warming land, the budding trees and plants. He cannot close his ears to the bird-songs that resound from orchard and woodland, from dooryard and pasture, from field and fen.

Nor can he close his ears and his heart to the glorious message of Easter as expressed in the hymns and from the pulpits of churches across the land. Each person becomes aware that there is something far greater than the accumulation of wealth and material things. He learns that all riches must be in faith and spirit and love. And with these truths before him, there is no longer room in his heart for greed and hate. There is room only for love and compassion, room only for peace and the richness of its content. Such is the message of Easter.

15

Photograph © DAJ/Getty Images, Inc.

Joyous Easter Season

ALICE M. STEWART

Joyous Easter season,
Resurrection time,
Pealing from church steeples
Hear the glad bells chime!
They ring out the story
Of the empty tomb.
Listen to their harmony
Dispersing winter's gloom.

Joyous Easter season . . .
Most blessed of the year.
Hear the choirs singing,
Voices pure and clear.
Hymn and anthem offer
Praise to Christ above
Who gave His life for others—
A sacrifice of love.

Joyous Easter season . . .
See the blossoms bright
Lift their smiling faces
Upward to the light,

Looking to the sunshine,
Knowing well it's true
Springtime and Eastertime
Wake the earth anew.

Joyous Easter season . . .
All things are made free;
Venturous birds returning
Broadcast melody.
Ardent little songsters
Flitting here and there,
Trilling out their message
That the world is fair.

Joyous Easter season . . .
The stone was rolled away.
Christ arose in triumph
To reign on high for aye.
May we, humble, reverent,
Grateful homage raise
And, our hearts rejoicing,
Join the songs of praise.

The Joys of Easter

EDITH HELSTERN

Let Easter joys be in your heart;
Let skies above be blue;
Then may your dearest
       hopes and dreams
Come swiftly, sweetly true.
And as the Easter days go by,
Let all their cheer remain
To echo always in your heart
In loving, glad refrain.

Easter Gladness

CAROLINE S. KOTOWICZ

With spring
Gladness will arrive.
Happy days will join
Easter fulfillment.
Faith will instill
Reverence.
The lily will grace
The power of His love;
His sunrise Resurrection
Brings peace.

A Tioga County United Methodist church in Ebenezer, Pennsylvania. Photograph © H. Mark Weidman Photography/Workbook Stock/Jupiter Images

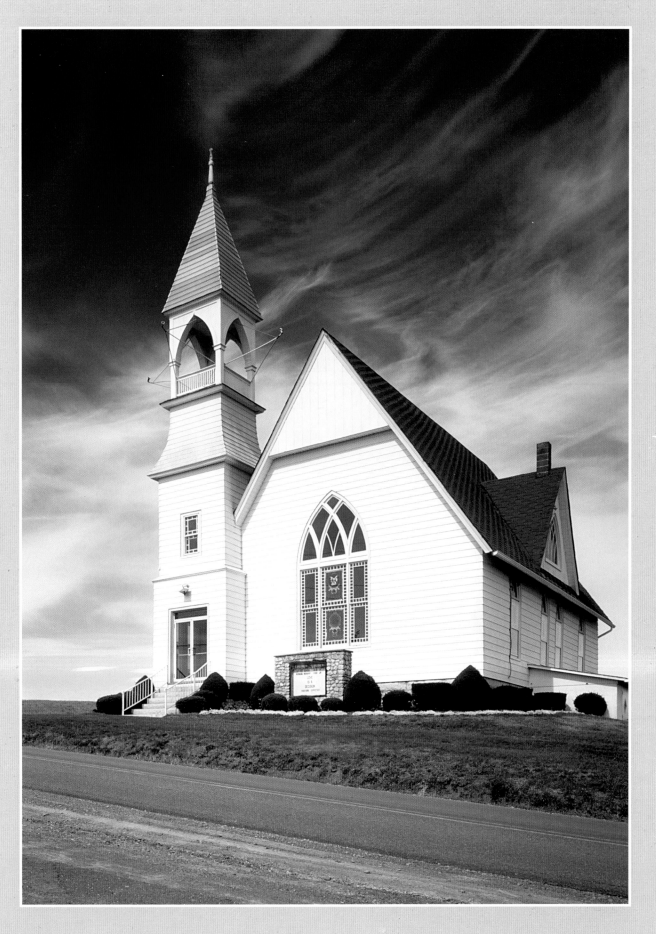

OUT OF NAZARETH

JOHN 1:19-46

And this is the record of John, when the Jews sent priests and Levites from Jerusalem to ask him, Who art thou?

And he confessed, and denied not; but confessed, I am not the Christ.

And they asked him, What then? Art thou Elias? And he saith, I am not. Art thou that prophet? And he answered, No. Then said they unto him, Who art thou? that we may give an answer to them that sent us. What sayest thou of thyself?

He said, I am the voice of one crying in the wilderness, Make straight the way of the Lord, as said the prophet Esaias.

And they which were sent were of the Pharisees. And they asked him, and said unto him, Why baptizest thou then, if thou be not that Christ, nor Elias, neither that prophet?

John answered them, saying, I baptize with water: but there standeth one among you, whom ye know not; He it is, who coming after me is preferred before me, whose shoe's latchet I am not worthy to unloose.

These things were done in Bethabara beyond Jordan, where John was baptizing.

The next day John seeth Jesus coming unto him, and saith, Behold the Lamb of God, which taketh away the sin of the world.

This is he of whom I said, After me cometh a man which is preferred before me: for he was before me. And I knew him not: but that he should be made manifest to Israel, therefore am I come baptizing with water.

And John bare record, saying, I saw the Spirit descending from heaven like a dove, and it abode upon him. And I knew him not: but he that sent me to baptize with water, the same said unto me, Upon whom thou shalt see the Spirit descending, and remaining on him, the same is he which baptizeth with the Holy Ghost. And I saw, and bare record that this is the Son of God.

Again the next day after John stood, and two of his disciples; And looking upon Jesus as he walked, he saith, Behold the Lamb of God!

And the two disciples heard him speak, and they followed Jesus. Then Jesus turned, and saw them following, and saith unto them, What seek ye? They said unto him, Rabbi, (which is to say, being interpreted, Master,) where dwellest thou?

He saith unto them, Come and see. They came and saw where he dwelt, and abode with him that day: for it was about the tenth hour.

One of the two which heard John speak, and followed him, was Andrew, Simon Peter's

ST. JOHN THE BAPTIST PREACHING *by Baciccio. Image © Scala/Art Resource, NY*

brother. He first findeth his own brother Simon, and saith unto him, We have found the Messias, which is, being interpreted, the Christ. And he brought him to Jesus. And when Jesus beheld him, he said, Thou art Simon the son of Jona: thou shalt be called Cephas, which is by interpretation, A stone.

The day following Jesus would go forth into Galilee, and findeth Philip, and saith unto him, Follow me. Now Philip was of Bethsaida, the city of Andrew and Peter.

Philip findeth Nathanael, and saith unto him, We have found him, of whom Moses in the law, and the prophets, did write, Jesus of Nazareth, the son of Joseph.

And Nathanael said unto him, Can there any good thing come out of Nazareth? Philip saith unto him, Come and see.

Renewal of the Soul

GERTRUDE RUDBERG

Easter is to everyone
Renewal of the soul
When spring bursts forth with songs of birds
After winter cold.

It fills our hearts with hopefulness;
Its promise is sublime
Of life renewed and souls restored
In every earthly clime.

It lights the way in caverns dark,
Where fear we've felt and seen,
And melts the frozen rivulets
Of doubting in between.

It paints the heavens bright with blue,
Embroiders them with lace,
Where we recall our risen Lord
Ascended to in grace.

21

An Easter Wish

JUNE MASTERS BACHER

The world springs up
All fresh and sweet,
With wings of faith
Upon its feet.

Would that each heart
Were more like it:
By hope made strong
And faith made fit

To reach toward God's
Eternal blue
With love that polishes
It like new—

A heart that hopes
And prays and sings
And soars by faith
On Easter wings.

Pink azaleas along the Blue Ridge Parkway in Virginia.
Photograph © Terry Donnelly/Austin Donnelly Photography

My Master Was So Very Poor

HARRY LEE

My Master was so very poor;
A manger was His cradling place.
So very rich my Master was;
Kings came from far to gain His grace.
My Master was so very poor;
And with the poor He broke the bread.
So very rich my Master was
That multitudes by Him were fed.
My Master was so very poor;
They nailed Him to a cross.
So very rich my Master was;
He gave His all and knew no loss.

Amid the Din of Earthly Strife

HENRY WARBURTON HAWKES

Amid the din of earthly strife,
Amid the busy crowd,
The whispers of eternal life
Are lost in clamors loud.
When lo! I find a healing balm,
The world grows dim to me;
My spirit rests in sudden calm
With Him of Galilee.
I linger near Him in the throng
And listen to His voice;
I feel my weary soul grow strong,
My saddened heart rejoice.
Amid the storms that darkly frown
I hear His call to me
And lay my heavy burden down
With Him of Galilee.

A synagogue where Jesus taught, Capernaum, Israel. Photograph © Jeff Greenberg/Grant Heilman Photography, Inc.

22

SET IN MOTION

Then when Mary was come where Jesus was, and saw him, she fell down at his feet, saying unto him, Lord, if thou hadst been here, my brother had not died.

When Jesus therefore saw her weeping, and the Jews also weeping which came with her, he groaned in the spirit, and was troubled. And said, Where have ye laid him? They said unto him, Lord, come and see. Jesus wept.

Then said the Jews, Behold how he loved him! And some of them said, Could not this man, which opened the eyes of the blind, have caused that even this man should not have died?

Jesus therefore again groaning in himself cometh to the grave. It was a cave, and a stone lay upon it. Jesus said, Take ye away the stone. Martha, the sister of him that was dead, saith unto him, Lord, by this time he stinketh: for he hath been dead four days.

Jesus saith unto her, Said I not unto thee, that, if thou wouldest believe, thou shouldest see the glory of God? Then they took away the stone from the place where the dead was laid. And Jesus lifted up his eyes, and said, Father, I thank thee that thou hast heard me. And I knew that thou hearest me always: but because of the people which stand by I said it, that they may believe that thou hast sent me. And when he thus had spoken, he cried with a loud voice, Lazarus, come forth.

And he that was dead came forth, bound hand and foot with graveclothes: and his face was bound about with a napkin. Jesus saith unto them, Loose him, and let him go.

Then many of the Jews which came to Mary, and had seen the things which Jesus did, believed on him. But some of them went their ways to the Pharisees, and told them what things Jesus had done. Then gathered the chief priests and the Pharisees a council, and said, What do we? for this man doeth many miracles. If we let him thus alone, all men will believe on him: and the Romans shall come and take away both our place and nation.

And one of them, named Caiaphas, being the high priest that same year, said unto them, Ye know nothing at all, Nor consider that it is expedient for us, that one man should die for the people, and that the whole nation perish not.

And this spake he not of himself: but being high priest that year, he prophesied that Jesus should die for that nation; And not for that nation only, but that also he should gather together in one the children of God that were scattered abroad. Then from that day forth they took counsel together for to put him to death.

THE RESURRECTION OF LAZARUS by *Geertgen tot Sint Jans. Image © Erich Lessing/Art Resource, NY*

From Bethlehem to Calvary

MEREDITH NICHOLSON

From Bethlehem to Calvary the Savior's journey lay;
Doubt, unbelief, scorn, fear, and hate beset Him day by day,
But in His heart He bore God's love that brightened all the way.

O'er the Judaean hills He walked, serene and brave of soul,
Seeking the beaten paths of men, touching and making whole,
Dying at last for love of man, on Calvary's darkened knoll.

He went with patient step and slow, as one who scatters seed;
Like a fierce hunger in His heart, He felt the world's great need,
And the negations Moses gave He changed to loving deed.

From Bethlehem to Calvary the world still follows on.
Even as the halt and blind of old along His path were drawn;
Through Calvary's clouds they seek the light that led Him to the dawn.

From Nazareth He Comes

RAYMOND KRESENSKY

From Nazareth He comes, the carpenter
Who knows of hammering and blows that break
The worker's hands. From Galilee He comes,
The fisherman who walks upon the lake.

Through fields of harvest, ripe for plucking grain;
Along the dusty roads that go beside
The vineyards, Christ, the noble carpenter,
Goes to the city to be crucified.

Jerusalem's streets are filled with those
Who cry, "Hosanna!" and others, "Crucify!"
For all of these He hangs upon the cross
That lifts itself into the purple sky.

For all of these the Master lived and died.
His lamp is tall and bright; our lamps are dim,
But we can see the way ahead of us,
For where the Master goes we go with Him.

Western shore of the Sea of Galilee. Photograph © Erich Lessing/Art Resource

AWAITING A SAVIOR

CROWDS AND CONFLICTS

KEN DUNCAN

The short years of Jesus' ministry featured a continual ebb and flow of popularity and animosity. At first, His charismatic presence attracted curious and adoring crowds. The rising tide of popularity seemed unstoppable. Those who opposed Jesus didn't fear Him; they feared the crowds. But there was always an undertow of doubt, fear, jealousy, and disagreement over His identity and power. Today's adoring crowd may turn into tomorrow's lynch mob. . . .

Followers and enemies walked with Jesus almost every day. As His influence grew, so did the desperation of those anxious to silence Him. They used various strategies, testing Him with questions and confronting Him with problems. At other times, as with the woman caught in adultery, they tried to force Jesus into compromise or failure. All these attempts fell short.

For weeks, Jesus moved steadily toward Jerusalem. He had traveled there before, but His journey had the look and feel of a final visit. He was moving in that direction spiritually as well as geographically. When Jesus told His disciples what would happen, they were conflicted. They resisted the idea of Jesus' death. How could He be the Messiah and yet die? How could He be king and not live to reign? How could someone so powerful be defeated and killed?

Jesus gave them clues and clear answers, but they remained unconvinced, unprepared, and troubled. Although the ominous future made them fear for their own lives, they continued to walk with Jesus. They didn't abandon Him—yet. Thomas seems to have expressed their inner turmoil with a unique flavor of resigned faithfulness with his statement, "Let us also go, that we may die with him" (John 11:16, NIV).

The walls of Old Jerusalem in Israel. Photograph
© Erich Lessing/Art Resource, NY

THE GLORY OF EASTER

Crown Him with Many Crowns

Matthew Bridges & Godfrey Thring

George J. Elvey

1. Crown Him with man - y crowns, The
2. Crown Him the Lord of life, Who
3. Crown Him the Lord of love! Be -

Lamb up - on His throne; Hark! How the heav'n - ly
tri - umphed o'er the grave, And 'rose vic - to - rious
hold His hands and side, Rich wounds, yet vis - i -

an - them drowns All mu - sic but its own! A -
in the strife For those He came to save; His
ble a - bove, In beau - ty glo - ri - fied: All

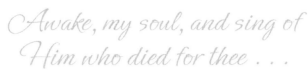

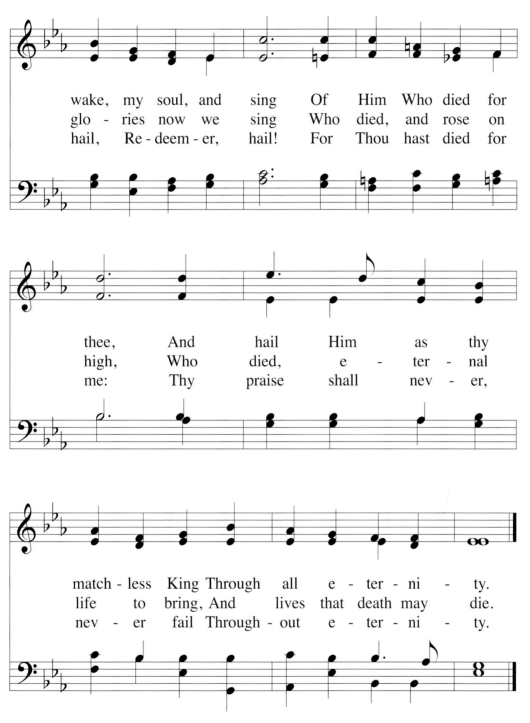

THE *Holy* WEEK

CHAPTER TWO

TRIUMPH AND TENSION

KEN DUNCAN

The air that morning seemed shot through with anticipation. Pilgrims on their way to Jerusalem for the Passover knew they would be in the city by nightfall. For many of them, this would be their first time in David's City. The traditional Psalms of Ascent were on everyone's lips. People were in a mood to praise God!

Then news spread through the crowd that Jesus the prophet, healer, and, some said, Messiah, was among them. Mounted on a young donkey, Jesus reminded many of the ancient tradition of kings riding on colts when they approached the great city in peace. The sign represented humility more than royalty. And that's why this entrance into Jerusalem was all the more triumphant—because His purpose wasn't triumph. Jesus had a victory of a different kind in mind—one that would require the ultimate sacrifice.

As we follow Jesus through Jerusalem, we soon realize that He walked there in our place, for our benefit. He took the painful steps that led to the cross—on our behalf. Isaiah described this process centuries earlier when he wrote, "But he was pierced for our transgressions, he was crushed for our iniquities; the punishment that brought us peace was upon him, and by his wounds we are healed" (Isaiah 53:5, NIV).

Jesus walked for us.

35

Damas Gate in Jerusalem, Israel. Photograph © Hemis.fr/SuperStock

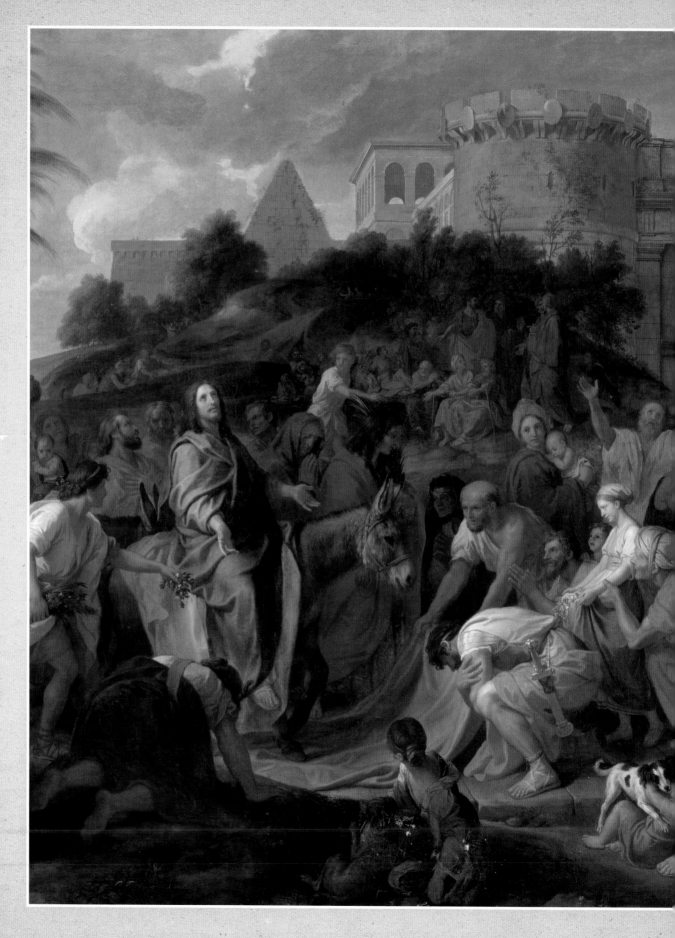

36

PALM SUNDAY

MARK 11:1-11

And when they came nigh to Jerusalem, unto Bethphage and Bethany, at the mount of Olives, he sendeth forth two of his disciples, And saith unto them, Go your way into the village over against you: and as soon as ye be entered into it, ye shall find a colt tied, whereon never man sat; loose him, and bring him. And if any man say unto you, Why do ye this? say ye that the Lord hath need of him; and straightway he will send him hither.

And they went their way, and found the colt tied by the door without in a place where two ways met; and they loose him.

And certain of them that stood there said unto them, What do ye, loosing the colt?

And they said unto them even as Jesus had commanded: and they let them go.

And they brought the colt to Jesus, and cast their garments on him; and he sat upon him. And many spread their garments in the way: and others cut down branches off the trees, and strawed them in the way.

And they that went before, and they that followed, cried, saying, Hosanna; Blessed is he that cometh in the name of the Lord: Blessed be the kingdom of our father David, that cometh in the name of the Lord: Hosanna in the highest.

And Jesus entered into Jerusalem, and into the temple: and when he had looked round about upon all things, and now the eventide was come, he went out unto Bethany with the twelve.

CHRIST'S ENTRY INTO JERUSALEM *by Charles Le Brun*.
Image © Réunion des Musées Nationaux/Art Resource, NY

37

They Cut the Branches
RAYMOND ORNER

They cut the branches from the trees
And strew them in the way
Because they knew their Lord and King
Would come along that day.

They sang Hosanna to the King
And praised His holy name;
Now even in this modern day,
We too should do the same.

The Christ who came that palm-strewn way
To enter in the gate
Will enter in your heart today,
So do not make Him wait.

That palm-strewn path of long ago
Is still a victory sign
That Christ still comes along the way
Into your heart and mine.

Palm Sunday
LAURIE E. DAWSON

I would have liked to walk along the way
And wave the branches green and gay;
To have caught a glimpse of the gentle face
As He rode that day with lowly grace.

I wish I could have sung His praise
And known about His kingly ways;
To have seen the love upon His face,
As He rode that day with measured pace.

I was not there, but still I know
The many ways that I can show
My love for others and keep today,
Palm Sunday, in my heart to stay.

Day of Palms
ALICE KENNELLY ROBERTS

Tomorrow is the day of palms
With triumph in the air,
A day to share Jerusalem
With memories everywhere,
A day to share Judean hills
And shores of Galilee,
To sense the shadow of a cross
And dark Gethsemane.

We ride again the rocky road
Two thousand years have worn.
We see again the cheering throngs
So soon to weep and mourn;
And all the troubles of this age,
Perplexing though they be,
Were felt upon that road of palms
Which led toward Calvary.

Tree in Jaffa, Israel. Photograph © National Geographic/SuperStock

THE HOLY WEEK.

THE UPPER ROOM

PETER MARSHALL

A sinister silence beat in upon the heavy hearts of a group of twelve men gathered in an upper room. They knew that something dreadful was about to happen and they were apprehensive.

This was the last night of Jesus' life on earth.

He had looked forward to this occasion, having His own apostles—His chosen friends, his intimate companions for three years—grouped around Him in the fellowship of the Last Supper.

He had Himself made the arrangements for the supper. "Look for a man carrying a pitcher of water," He had told His disciples. That in itself would be an unusual thing, for it was the women who usually carried the water.

The man would lead them to this upper room, perhaps in the home of John Mark's father—a guest room built on the flat roof of the house. . . .

The men were reclining on couches around a low U-shaped table. At the Master's left was Simon Peter . . . at His right, John.

A quiet voice spoke: "With desire I have desired to eat this passover with you before I suffer. . . ." Bronzed hands took a loaf of bread, gave thanks for it, broke it. "This is My body which is given for you: this do in remembrance of Me."

The Last Supper was to institute a memorial—the loving desire to be remembered. Christ relied upon homely symbols—a piece of bread, a cup of the juice of the lowly grape—to recall Him to future generations. He knew that we would be in constant danger of forgetting Him, therefore He enlisted sense on the side of faith and trusted to these simple memorials for the recalling to our treacherous memories of His undying love.

"This is the blood of the new testament—a new agreement—which is shed for many for the remission of sins. Drink ye all of it. . . . But I say unto you, I will not drink henceforth of this fruit of the vine until that day when I drink it new with you in My Father's kingdom."

Strange words with which to institute a sacrament. What did He mean?

40

Stained glass in Holy Trinity Cathedral, Addis Ababa, Ethiopia. Photograph © Gavin Hellier/Robert Harding/Jupiter Images

The words that fell from His lips that night are standing evidence of Christ's own estimate as to where the center of His work lies—We are to remember His death. Never did He ask that we should commemorate His birth. Not once did He request that any of the wonderful deeds He performed should be immortalized. Only this—His last and greatest work—the work of redemption.

This was to be His memorial—a cross—to remind us that God's love for us is a love that hate cannot nullify and death cannot kill. Already, days before, He had told His apostles: "Behold, we go up to Jerusalem . . . the Son of Man . . . shall be mocked, and spitefully entreated . . . and they shall scourge Him, and put Him to death; and the third day He shall rise again. . . ."

THE HOLY WEEK

THE LAST SUPPER

Now the feast of unleavened bread drew nigh, which is called the Passover. And the chief priests and scribes sought how they might kill him; for they feared the people.

Then entered Satan into Judas surnamed Iscariot, being of the number of the twelve. And he went his way, and communed with the chief priests and captains, how he might betray him unto them. And they were glad, and covenanted to give him money. And he promised, and sought opportunity to betray him unto them in the absence of the multitude.

Then came the day of unleavened bread, when the passover must be killed. And he sent Peter and John, saying, Go and prepare us the passover, that we may eat.

And they said unto him, Where wilt thou that we prepare?

And he said unto them, Behold, when ye are entered into the city, there shall a man meet you, bearing a pitcher of water; follow him into the house where he entereth in. And ye shall say unto the goodman of the house, The Master saith unto thee, Where is the guestchamber, where I shall eat the passover with my disciples? And he shall shew you a large upper room furnished: there make ready.

And they went, and found as he had said unto them: and they made ready the passover.

And when the hour was come, he sat down, and the twelve apostles with him.

And he said unto them, With desire I have desired to eat this passover with you before I suffer: For I say unto you, I will not any more eat thereof, until it be fulfilled in the kingdom of God. And he took the cup, and gave thanks, and said, Take this, and divide it among yourselves: For I say unto you, I will not drink of the fruit of the vine, until the kingdom of God shall come.

And he took bread, and gave thanks, and brake it, and gave unto them, saying, This is my body which is given for you: this do in remembrance of me. Likewise also the cup after supper, saying, This cup is the new testament in my blood, which is shed for you.

But, behold, the hand of him that betrayeth me is with me on the table. And truly the Son of man goeth, as it was determined: but woe unto that man by whom he is betrayed!

And they began to enquire among themselves, which of them it was that should do this thing. And there was also a strife among them, which of them should be accounted the greatest.

And he said unto them, The kings of the Gentiles exercise lordship over them; and they

42

THE LAST SUPPER *by Vincente Macip I. Image © SuperStock, Inc./SuperStock*

that exercise authority upon them are called benefactors. But ye shall not be so: but he that is greatest among you, let him be as the younger; and he that is chief, as he that doth serve.

For whether is greater, he that sitteth at meat, or he that serveth? is not he that sitteth at meat? but I am among you as he that serveth. Ye are they which have continued with me in my temptations. And I appoint unto you a kingdom, as my Father hath appointed unto me; That ye may eat and drink at my table in my kingdom, and sit on thrones judging the twelve tribes of Israel.

And the Lord said, Simon, Simon, behold, Satan hath desired to have you, that he may sift you as wheat: But I have prayed for thee, that thy faith fail not: and when thou art converted, strengthen thy brethren.

And he said unto him, Lord, I am ready to go with thee, both into prison, and to death.

And he said, I tell thee, Peter, the cock shall not crow this day, before that thou shalt thrice deny that thou knowest me.

And he said unto them, When I sent you without purse, and scrip, and shoes, lacked ye any thing? And they said, Nothing.

Then said he unto them, But now, he that hath a purse, let him take it, and likewise his scrip: and he that hath no sword, let him sell his garment, and buy one.

For I say unto you, that this that is written must yet be accomplished in me, And he was reckoned among the transgressors: for the things concerning me have an end.

And they said, Lord, behold, here are two swords. And he said unto them, It is enough.

In the Upper Room

HELEN WELSHIMER

Perhaps at first they talked of little things
At suppertime that evening in the spring.
The upper room was dim with candle-shine
As Jesus sat with twelve, remembering.
Then quietly He said, "There is one here
Whose kiss will bring betrayal by and by."
They did not look at Judas curiously,
But each man murmured, "Master, is it I?"

Each one looked inward, frightened lest he find
A shoddy place where he had dreamed of steel.
None placed the guilt on any other guest
Who had partaken of that gracious meal.
When there are hungry on my little street,
When I see tears or hear a heart's hurt cry
Because someone has failed to keep high faith,
May I, too, murmur, "Master, is it I?"

The Door

HAROLD C. BONELL

Gladly they entered and the door swung to;
Not so much that the world was shut outside,
But that inside the room there could abide
The warmth and friendship of the faithful few.
Then, in the circle of the candles' light,
They took the wine and the unleavened bread
And prayerfully the ancient ritual said,
All safe behind the door that holy night.

The door swung open when the feast was done
To send them out to face what was in store;
The will of God hides not behind a door,
And, prayer completed, life has just begun.

Go forth in faith from every place of prayer;
The challenges of life are waiting there.

*Room commemorating the room of the Last
Supper, just outside the walls of Old Jerusalem
in Israel. Photograph © Jean Conte*

The Last Supper

WILLIAM ARNETTE WOFFORD

45

Now when the eventide was come
With shadows deepening into gloom,
Came Jesus with the twelve and sat
At supper in the upper room.

A solemn hush fell over them;
And in the soft gold candlelight,
His heart was heavy, for He knew
His hour was near at hand that night.

And while they ate, He reverently
Began to bless and break the bread.
"This is My body given for you;
Take ye and eat," the Master said.

He took the cup, and giving thanks,
He gave it to them lovingly.
"This is My blood, drink ye of it;
Do this in memory of Me."

They would remember all their lives
The poignant beauty in His face
And treasure too the blessed words
He spoke there in that quiet place.

Gethsemane

MARGARET E. SANGSTER

The dew lay thick on thorn and flower,
And where the olives clustered gray
Weird shapes within that awesome hour
Between the midnight and the day
Seemed walking phantom-like abroad,
As if to vex the Son of God.
And all the city lay asleep,
O'er beast and bird the spell was cast.
And nothing stirred the silence deep,
Save where our Lord the vigil passed,
The long lone vigil when His prayer
Was uttered from a heart's despair.
"Oh, watch with me one little hour!"
His tender tones had pleading cried
Unto the faithful three whose dower
Of love had kept them near His side.
Nay—folded hands and drooping head,
And slumber—quiet as the dead.
No wonder then for weariness
The second time they fall asleep,
He turns in very tenderness
And leaves them to repose so deep.
Alone He meets the serpent foe;
Alone He bears the bitter woe.

Gethsemane! Gethsemane!
We see the glory and the gloom!
Through all thy pain and agony,
Thy garden wears immortal bloom.
'Twas human friendship failed Him there,
But love divine did hear His prayer.
Life's bitter cups we too must take,
Life's bitter bread in anguish eat.
But when our hearts are like to break
There comes to us a whisper sweet,
"Fear thou no dim Gethsemane;
Thy sleepless Friend will watch with thee!"

Linville Gorge, North Carolina. Photograph © Carr Clifton

46

THE KISS OF JUDAS by Cornelis Engebrechtsz. Image © Musee Denon, Chalon-sur-Saone,
France/Roger-Viollet, Paris/The Bridgeman Art Library

Betrayal in the Garden

And he came out, and went, as he was wont, to the mount of Olives; and his disciples also followed him. And when he was at the place, he said unto them, Pray that ye enter not into temptation. And he was withdrawn from them about a stone's cast, and kneeled down, and prayed, Saying, Father, if thou be willing, remove this cup from me: nevertheless not my will, but thine, be done. And there appeared an angel unto him from heaven, strengthening him.

And being in an agony he prayed more earnestly: and his sweat was as it were great drops of blood falling down to the ground.

And when he rose up from prayer, and was come to his disciples, he found them sleeping for sorrow, And said unto them, Why sleep ye? rise and pray, lest ye enter into temptation.

And while he yet spake, behold a multitude, and he that was called Judas, one of the twelve, went before them, and drew near unto Jesus to kiss him. But Jesus said unto him, Judas, betrayest thou the Son of man with a kiss?

When they which were about him saw what would follow, they said unto him, Lord, shall we smite with the sword? And one of them smote the servant of the high priest, and cut off his right ear. And Jesus answered and said, Suffer ye thus far. And he touched his ear, and healed him.

Then Jesus said unto the chief priests, and captains of the temple, and the elders, which were come to him, Be ye come out, as against a thief, with swords and staves? When I was daily with you in the temple, ye stretched forth no hands against me: but this is your hour, and the power of darkness. Then took they him, and led him, and brought him into the high priest's house. And Peter followed afar off.

And when they had kindled a fire in the midst of the hall, and were set down together, Peter sat down among them. But a certain maid beheld him as he sat by the fire, and earnestly looked upon him, and said, This man was also with him. And he denied him, saying, Woman, I know him not. And after a little while another saw him, and said, Thou art also of them. And Peter said, Man, I am not. And about the space of one hour after another confidently affirmed, saying, Of a truth this fellow also was with him: for he is a Galilaean. And Peter said, Man, I know not what thou sayest. And immediately, while he yet spake, the cock crew.

And the Lord turned, and looked upon Peter. And Peter remembered the word of the Lord, how he had said unto him, Before the cock crow, thou shalt deny me thrice.

And Peter went out, and wept bitterly.

I Was There

Kenneth Chafin

*N*one of my earliest memories of Holy Week are religious. They're of watching my mother sew a new dress for my sister or color boiled eggs with bluing or food coloring. One year I stood on a piece of paper, and she traced the outline of my foot and had our neighbor bring me new shoes from town. They were too tight, but I didn't mention it for fear she would send them back.

When I was nine, my folks moved from the farm to an industrial community in northern Illinois, and my grandmother enrolled me in a Sunday school class at a nearby church. A very caring woman taught it. That first spring she guided my study of the story of the Crucifixion. I remember thinking, If Jesus had only come today, I'm sure that I wouldn't have treated Him that way. I think my child's heart was completely sincere, but I've come to doubt that Jesus would have been treated any differently in our—or any—time.

If someone came to us preaching a God who is defined by compassion, spent time with people we look down on, encouraged people not to keep all the rules religion has developed and demanded that we radically remake our lives, our sins would cry out to silence that one. The cross was inevitable.

It hurts me to admit it, but it's true: there is a little bit of each of the people of that first Holy Week in me. So when I hear again the words of the spiritual, "Were you there when they crucified my Lord?" I know that the answer is "Yes, I was there. In God's love and in my sin. And that fact makes all the difference in my life."

Dogwood blossoms in DeSoto State Park, Alabama.
Photograph by William H. Johnson

A Ballad of Trees and the Master

SIDNEY LANIER

Into the woods my Master went,
Clean, forspent, forspent.
Into the woods my Master came,
Forspent with love and shame,
But the olives they were not blind to Him,
The little gray leaves were kind to Him:
The thorn-tree had a mind to Him
When into the woods He came.

Out of the woods my Master went,
And He was well content.
Out of the woods my Master came,
Content with death and shame.
When Death and Shame would woo Him last,
From under the trees they drew Him last:
'Twas on a tree they slew Him—last
When out of the woods He came.

53

*This day upon the
bitter tree died One
who, had He willed,
could have dried up
the wide sea and
the wind stilled.*

—A. J. M. SMITH

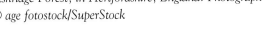

*Ashridge Forest, in Hertfordshire, England. Photograph
© age fotostock/SuperStock*

The Crucifixion

Matthew 27:33-54

And when they were come unto a place called Golgotha, that is to say, a place of a skull, They gave him vinegar to drink mingled with gall: and when he had tasted thereof, he would not drink.

And they crucified him, and parted his garments, casting lots: that it might be fulfilled which was spoken by the prophet, They parted my garments among them, and upon my vesture did they cast lots. And sitting down they watched him there; And set up over his head his accusation written, THIS IS JESUS THE KING OF THE JEWS.

Then were there two thieves crucified with him, one on the right hand, and another on the left. And they that passed by reviled him, wagging their heads, And saying, Thou that destroyest the temple, and buildest it in three days, save thyself. If thou be the Son of God, come down from the cross.

Likewise also the chief priests mocking him, with the scribes and elders, said, He saved others; himself he cannot save. If he be the King of Israel, let him now come down from the cross, and we will believe him. He trusted in God; let him deliver him now, if he will have him: for he said, I am the Son of God.

The thieves also, which were crucified with him, cast the same in his teeth. Now from the sixth hour there was darkness over all the land unto the ninth hour.

And about the ninth hour Jesus cried with a loud voice, saying, Eli, Eli, lama sabachthani? that is to say, My God, my God, why hast thou forsaken me?

Some of them that stood there, when they heard that, said, This man calleth for Elias. And straightway one of them ran, and took a sponge, and filled it with vinegar, and put it on a reed, and gave him to drink. The rest said, Let be, let us see whether Elias will come to save him.

Jesus, when he had cried again with a loud voice, yielded up the ghost.

And, behold, the veil of the temple was rent in twain from the top to the bottom; and the earth did quake, and the rocks rent; And the graves were opened; and many bodies of the saints which slept arose, And came out of the graves after his resurrection, and went into the holy city, and appeared unto many.

Now when the centurion, and they that were with him, watching Jesus, saw the earthquake, and those things that were done, they feared greatly, saying, Truly this was the Son of God.

Calvary by Jan the Elder Brueghel. Image © Scala/Art Resource, NY

THE CROSS SHOWS ME THE JOY OF JESUS

NANCY GUTHRIE

He was willing to die a shameful death on the cross because of the joy he knew would be his afterward. —HEBREWS 12:2 (NLT)

What joy could Jesus see that enabled Him to endure the pain and agony of the cross? What joy did He know would be His? As Jesus looked ahead, He could see the joy of redemption. By paying the debt for sin, Jesus satisfied justice. It brought Him joy to complete the work He was sent to do, which was to pay the price for your sin and my sin. And as He endured the cross, your face was on His mind, and He was full of joy that the price was now paid so you could spend eternity with Him.

Jesus also anticipated the joy of Resurrection. He had told His followers numerous times that He would die and that He would also rise again. But they could not imagine the death, nor could they fathom resurrection. His was a shameful death—but not because of His own shame. He had never done anything to be ashamed of. He took the shame of everyone who has ever regretted things they have said or done. Yet Jesus could have true joy because He knew He would break the power of shame and death forever and offer abundant life. . . .

Occasionally we see on television the return of soldiers who have been away from their families for months or years at a time. And as we watch them run toward those they love, we can feel the sense of joy and release of their reunion, can't we? Now imagine Jesus, who lived in perfect fellowship with the Father from before the foundation of the world. Then He was sent to earth and took on human flesh, with work to do. And as Jesus headed toward the cross, He began to anticipate the joy of reunion with the Father. Jesus returned to heaven having endured the cross and completed the work. . . .

But Jesus is not content to keep this joy to Himself. He longs to share His joy with you and me—as we are redeemed and as we anticipate resurrection—when we will be reunited with Him forever. What joy!

Rickett's Glen Park in Scranton, Pennsylvania. Photograph © Comstock/SuperStock

Were You There?

AUTHOR UNKNOWN

1. Were you there when they cru - ci - fied my
2. Were you there when they nailed Him to the
3. Were you there when they laid Him in the
4. Were you there when He rose up from the

Lord?   Were you there when they
tree?   Were you there when they
tomb?   Were you there when they
dead?   Were you there when He

cru - ci - fied my Lord?
nailed Him to the tree?
laid Him in the tomb?
rose up from the dead?

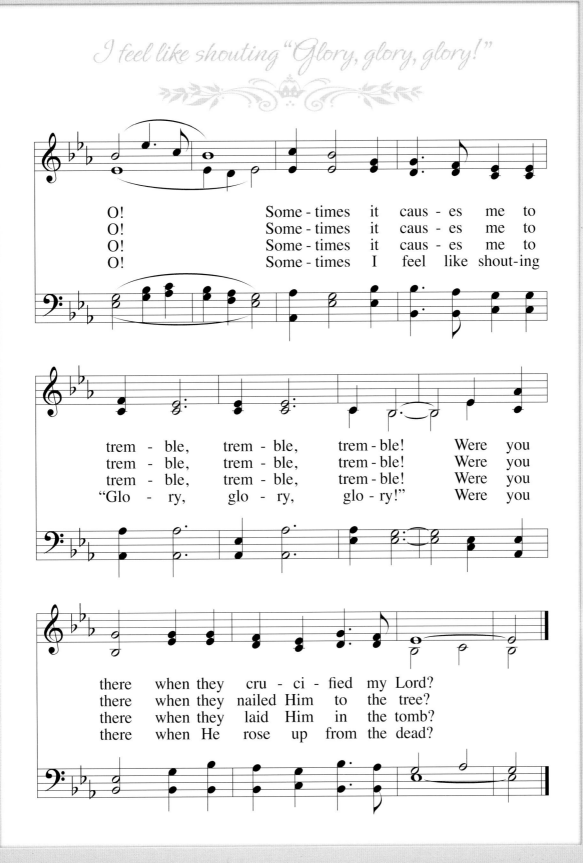

O!   Some-times it caus-es me to
O!   Some-times it caus-es me to
O!   Some-times it caus-es me to
O!   Some-times I feel like shout-ing

trem - ble, trem - ble, trem - ble! Were you
trem - ble, trem - ble, trem - ble! Were you
trem - ble, trem - ble, trem - ble! Were you
"Glo - ry, glo - ry, glo - ry!" Were you

there when they cru - ci - fied my Lord?
there when they nailed Him to the tree?
there when they laid Him in the tomb?
there when He rose up from the dead?

Golgotha's Hill

M. MAE FISHER

My Savior climbed Golgotha's hill,
Bearing His heavy load.
As painfully He upward toiled
Along that uphill road,
Great drops of sweat and drops of blood
Dripped for a cause sublime.
The cross He bore, the thorns He wore
Were His; the sins were mine!

They nailed Him to the cross of pain,
And there He died to win
The evil, stubborn hearts of men
And save them from their sin.
He laid His life, a bridge across,
Whereon we all may pass
Unto the Father's loving arms
To be redeemed at last.

Day of Sorrows

ALICE KENNELLY ROBERTS

The day of sorrows now has come,
A day of grief and loss,
A day when He who knew no sin
Was burdened with a cross.

We see Him fail beneath its weight
And toil the mountain road
Till steps forth Simon of Cyrene
To help Him bear the load.

We see the crown of thorns He wore;
We hear the frenzied throng;
We feel the hours of suffering
Which bore His soul along.

The nails, the words, the Roman guards
Mixed victory with loss
To write for all the centuries
The story of the cross.

Good Friday

CHRISTINA ROSSETTI

Am I a stone, and not a sheep,
    That I can stand, O Christ, beneath Thy cross,
To number drop by drop Thy blood's slow loss,
And yet not weep?

Not so those women loved
    Who with exceeding grief lamented Thee;
Not so fallen Peter weeping bitterly;
    Not so the thief was moved;

Not so the Sun and Moon
    Which hid their faces in a starless sky,
A horror of great darkness at broad noon—
    I, only I.

Yet give not o'er,
    But seek Thy sheep, true Shepherd of the flock;
Greater than Moses, turn and look once more
    And smite a rock.

Mount Rainier National Park, Washington.
Photograph © Tomas Kaspar

DARKEST BEFORE DAWN

He himself bore
our sins in his body on
the tree, so that we
might die to sins and
live for righteousness;
by his wounds you
have been healed.
—1 PETER 2:24 (NIV)

*S*till as of old
Men by themselves are priced—
For thirty pieces Judas sold
Himself, not Christ.
—HESTER H. CHOLMONDELEY

Could life so end,
half told; its school so fail?
Soul, soul, there is a sequel
to thy tale!
—ROBERT MOWRY BELL

*A*ll those who journey, soon or late,
Must pass within the garden gate;
Must kneel alone in darkness there
And battle with some fierce despair.
God pity those who cannot say:
"Not mine but thine"; who only pray:
"Let this cup pass" and cannot see
The purpose in Gethsemane.
—ELLA WHEELER WILCOX

In the bonds of death He lay
Who for our offense was slain;
But the Lord is risen today,
Christ hath brought us life again,
Wherefore let us all rejoice,
Singing loud, with cheerful voice,
Hallelujah!
—MARTIN LUTHER

The hands of Christ
Seem very frail,
For they were broken
By a nail.
But only they
Reach heaven at last
Whom these frail, broken
Hands hold fast.
—JOHN RICHARD MORELAND

We may not know, we cannot tell what pains He had to bear,
But we believe it was for us He hung and suffered there.
—CECIL F. ALEXANDER

What comfort by Him do we win
Who made Himself the price of sin
To make us heirs of glory?
To see this Babe, all innocence,
A martyr born in our defense:
Can man forget this story?
—BEN JONSON

Hail, Day of days! in peals of praise
Throughout all ages owned,
When Christ, our God, hell's empire trod,
And high o'er heaven was throned.
—SAINT VENANTIUS HONORIUS FORTUNATUS

*Where man sees but withered leaves,
God sees sweet flowers growing.*
—ALBERT LAIGHTON

Holy Saturday
John Banister Tabb

O Earth, who daily kissed His feet
Like lowly Magdalen—how sweet
(As oft His mother used) to keep
The silent watches of His sleep,
Till love demands the Prisoner,
And Death replies, "He is not here.
He passed my portal, where, afraid,
My footsteps faltered to invade
The region that beyond me lies:
Then, ere the dawn, I saw Him rise
In glory that dispelled my gloom
And made a temple of the tomb."

65

Our Christ
Harry Webb Farrington

I know not how that Bethlehem's Babe
Could in the God-head be;
I only know the manger Child
Has brought God's life to me.

I know not how that Calvary's cross
A world from sin could free:
I only know its matchless love
Has brought God's love to me.

I know not how that Joseph's tomb
Could solve death's mystery:
I only know a living Christ,
Our immortality.

Shenandoah National Park, Virginia. Photograph
© Mary Liz Austin/Austin Donnelly Photography

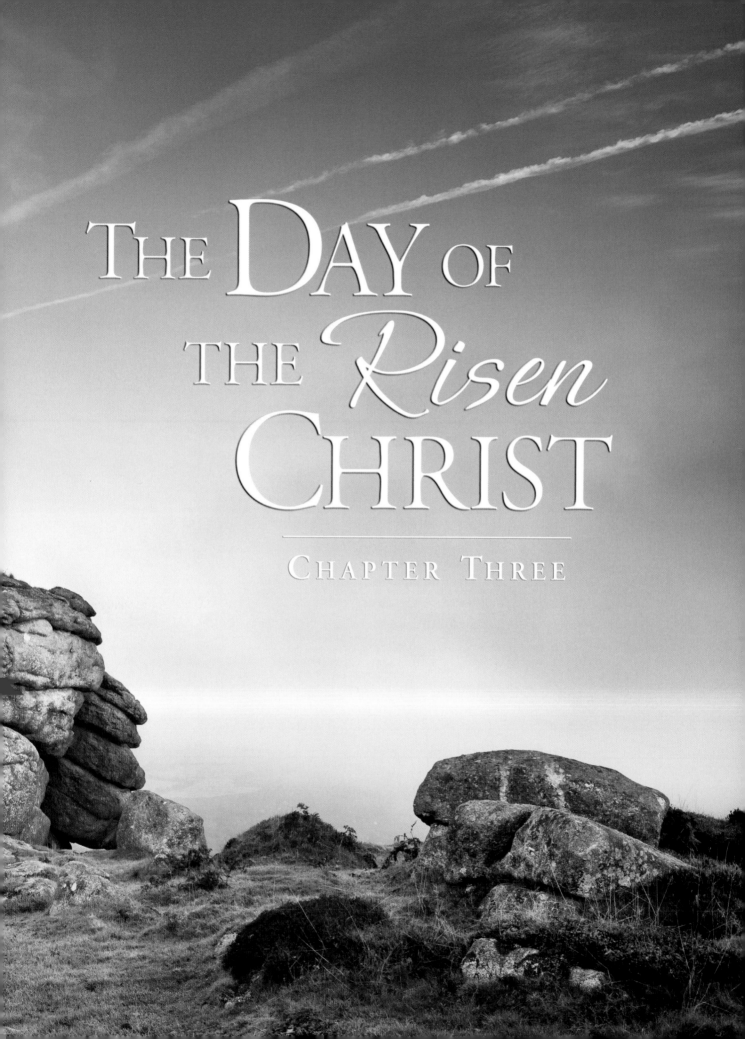

THE DAY OF THE RISEN CHRIST

CHAPTER THREE

Easter Chorus from Faust

JOHANN WOLFGANG VON GOETHE
TR. ARTHUR CLEVELAND COXE

Christ is arisen.
    Joy to thee, mortal!
Out of His prison,
    Forth from its portal!
Christ is not sleeping—
    Seek Him no longer.
Strong was His keeping;
    Jesus was stronger.

Christ is arisen.
    Seek Him not here;
Lonely His prison,
    Empty His bier;

Vain His entombing,
    Spices and lawn,
Vain the performing—
    Jesus is gone.

Christ is arisen.
    Joy to thee, mortal!
Empty His prison,
    Broken its portal!
Rising, He giveth
    His shroud to the sod;
Risen, He liveth,
    And liveth to God.

Easter Hymn

HENRY VAUGHAN

Death and darkness get you packing,
Nothing now to man is lacking;
All your triumphs now are ended,
And what Adam marred is mended.
Graves are beds now for the weary,
Death a nap, to wake more merry;
Youth now, full of pious duty,
Seeks in thee for perfect beauty.
The weak and aged, tir'd with length
Of days, from thee look for new strength;
And infants with thy pangs contest
As pleasant, as if with the breast.
Then, unto Him, who thus hath thrown
Even to contempt thy kingdom down,
And by His blood did us advance
Unto His own inheritance,
To Him be glory, power, praise
From this unto the last of days!

Fish Lake in Oregon. Photograph © Dennis Frates

THAT RESURRECTION MORN

CYNTHIA PEARL MAUS

When the darkness that followed the earthquake attending the death of Jesus had lifted from the land, the Nazarene was dead. "Strange," they said, "that He should so soon lose His mortal life." For among those who had watched His suffering, there were some who were actually offended because His sensitive and exhausted frame could no longer support His torture. Even in death He robbed His tormentors of much of their frenzied satisfaction. Taking the quickest possible steps to make sure that He was really dead, they hurried to Pilate with their urgent request. "Give us a guard for the tomb," they said, "for this Galilean made strange statements that He would rise from the dead on the third day. So give us guards," they demanded, "that His friends may not steal away His body, thereby saving His reputation as a prophet, and maintaining His hold on the imagination of the people."

And Pilate, already disgusted and weary of the subject because of the chiding of his wife, granted their request, gave them guards, and ordered that His tomb be sealed with the imperial seal of Rome.

No sooner had His persecutors departed than Joseph of Arimathea, a prominent Jew who had always loved the Rabbi in silence, pushed his influential claims demanding the dead body of the Nazarene, and offered his own new tomb, which had never been occupied, as the burial place. This eminent citizen achieved what His lowly disciples could not have accomplished.

With trembling fingers His chosen friends hurriedly drew the spikes out of His hands and feet, and with winding-sheets lowered His bruised and bleeding body to the ground. The tears of the woman who loved Him dashed upon His face as His head rested for a moment in the lap of His mother, while others of the more venturesome women lifted His bruised hands, that had healed and blessed but never harmed, to their lips. But His brow was so majestic in death that they could not intrude upon its now peaceful repose.

In the fast-fading light of the dying day they bore His body to the tomb with His beloved disciples as bearers and a few of the women following. Rudely they embalmed

His body in such spices as could hastily be pro-cured; and folding it into sweet, clean linen, left it in the outer chamber of this new tomb because there was not time for the final interment.

Hurriedly they rolled the entry-stone into its place as the sun sank and departed for their lonely and sad observance of the high Sabbath of holy week, just as the Roman guard supplied by Pilate came up to seal the tomb and begin their all-night vigil of this dead King of the Jews.

The night watchers were brave men and accustomed to grave duties, but they were uncomfortable, for strange rumors about His majesty in suffering had already come to their ears. The night was long and there was no wind. They talked quietly concerning His hurried trial and crucifixion, while within the vault, Jesus of Nazareth lay in state, awaiting the Resurrection morn.

When the night died away and the first streaks of dawn began to pale the Eastern sky, the watchmen passed to and fro, as was their wont, coming together at the mouth of the sepulcher, where they stood guard. Suddenly the face of one of the watchers blanched in terror as he pointed with his spear and then fell. The stone that closed the tomb was moving!

The other guard sprang, with an oath, and struck at the stone with his sword, but it missed. The great disk continued to move in its groove and rolled slowly off to one side.

The moon was gone and the sun had not yet risen, yet the garden glowed with a strange, transcendent light as if aflame with a sky-born glory. The bolder of the guards turned faint, as had his mate, and dropped beside him, as a regal form clothed in glowing white emerged from the tomb into the garden that surrounded it and disappeared in the misty light of that first Easter morn.

Later Mary, the Magdalene, came to the garden at Sunday's dawn. She had not slept, and she wondered why she could no longer weep. Somehow she thought of her miserable past without a pang. With wild joy she remembered what the Master had done for her. Other women had ministered unto Him, and loved Him: let them continue to mourn! They had not suffered as she had. In that hour she felt as if she had outloved them all—as, indeed, she had outrun them all in her desire to come first to the garden of His tomb.

She crept up on tiptoe, as one does who hesitates to disturb a dear slumberer, but stopped abruptly. The guards were nowhere to be seen. The stone was rolled away from the mouth of the tomb, and the sepulcher seemed open and empty. With her hands upon her heart, Mary gave one glance, then sped out of the garden and off to the lodgings of Peter and the other disciple whom Jesus loved, with her tragic message: "Our Lord is stolen from the tomb, and none to tell where He is borne away!"

Her breath was gone, and with it her courage also. She came back falteringly. She could not keep up with John and Peter, who ran on without noticing that she followed. When she reached the tomb they had already gone to share the tragic news of His disappearance with others who loved Him. Having no heart to go elsewhere, she loitered sadly about the deserted garden.

Meanwhile other women who had witnessed His tragic death came up more deliberately with their myrrh and spices, thinking to finish the burial preparations that their Sabbath law had interrupted, and to do for their Lord what should be done before it was too late. When they saw that the great stone had been rolled away, they put the myrrh carefully down on the ground and, stooping, crept into the open tomb. With shaking hands they reverently examined the grave-clothes and the linen face-cloth folded so carefully by itself. "He is not here," they said. And they, too, hurried away to spread the sad news that His body had been stolen from the tomb.

Mary Magdalene, who had been weeping silently in the garden, was alone again. Wearily she approached the open sepulcher; and, gathering her courage and strength, she stooped down and looked into the tomb for herself. The marble slab, on which His body had lain in state, was bare. Beyond was the crypt in which they had meant to inter Him today. The morning sun streamed in. The sepulcher seemed empty! But was it? Look again! At the head and foot on that long white marble slab, brilliant forms began to emerge, and she saw clearly through her tears the forms of two messengers clad in raiment of white.

Her tears ran into a sudden childlike smile, as she said to them: "They have taken away my Lord, and I know not where they have laid Him." Suddenly a shadow fell over her shoulder and entered the tomb. It was the shadowy figure of a man. She thought it was the keeper of the burial garden and began to explain to Him how and why she was there.

Sobs racked her body now so that her words were hardly coherent or articulate and her eyes were blinded by tears she could not restrain. She did not recognize the Stranger while she tried to tell Him of her heart-breaking disappointment in finding the tomb empty, until He called her by her own name.

Then a cry of wild joy went up to the morning skies that arched the dome above the tomb—a cry of joy that has rung its radiant message down through the centuries:

"Rabboni! Lord! My Lord! Dear, dear Lord!"

She sprang toward Him, crying and laughing, and her words fell from her in hysterical joy. "It is my dear Lord! *He is alive!*"

She fell at His feet and stretched up her arms to clasp Him, but He motioned her back, saying, "Touch Me not, for I have not yet ascended unto My Father, and to your Father, unto My God and your God. But go yonder into Jerusalem, and tell My disciples that I go before you to Galilee, there shall ye see Me, even as I have said. Mary! I am the Resurrection and the Life. He that believeth in Me though he were dead, yet shall he live; and he that liveth and believeth in Me shall never die!"

With unspeakable joy Mary Magdalene hurried away to bring her reassuring message to His disciples and to the world: "He is alive forevermore!"

Easter Promise
HELEN WILLIAMS

Remember that although the world
Once witnessed Friday's cross,
The promised joy of Easter came
To end that night of loss;
So that the Resurrection morn
Would never fail to be
The light of life that always robs
The grave of victory.

75

An Easter Song
SUSAN COOLIDGE

A song of sunshine through the rain,
Of spring across the snow;
A balm to heal the hurts of pain,
A peace surpassing woe.
Lift up your heads, ye sorrowing ones,
And be ye glad at heart.
For Calvary and Easter Day,
Earth's saddest day and gladdest day,
Were just three days apart!

*Blooming pear orchard near Mount Hood in the Hood
River Valley, Oregon. Photograph © Dennis Frates*

THE RESURRECTION

Now upon the first day of the week, very early in the morning, they came unto the sepulchre, bringing the spices which they had prepared, and certain others with them. And they found the stone rolled away from the sepulchre. And they entered in, and found not the body of the Lord Jesus.

And it came to pass, as they were much perplexed thereabout, behold, two men stood by them in shining garments: And as they were afraid, and bowed down their faces to the earth, they said unto them, Why seek ye the living among the dead? He is not here, but is risen: remember how he spake unto you when he was yet in Galilee, Saying, The Son of man must be delivered into the hands of sinful men, and be crucified, and the third day rise again.

And they remembered his words, And returned from the sepulchre, and told all these things unto the eleven, and to all the rest.

It was Mary Magdalene and Joanna, and Mary the mother of James, and other women that were with them, which told these things unto the apostles. And their words seemed to them as idle tales, and they believed them not.

Then arose Peter, and ran unto the sepulchre; and stooping down, he beheld the linen clothes laid by themselves, and departed, wondering in himself at that which was come to pass.

RESURRECTION OF CHRIST. *Florentine School. Image ©*
Erich Lessing/Art Resource, NY

THE DAY OF THE RISEN CHRIST

Christ Is Risen

GRACE NOLL CROWELL

Often through life we have our own dark garden:
Our own Gethsemane,
With no hint at all of an early springtime morning,
Silvering bush and tree.
Then suddenly a startling cry is lifting
To meet our desperate need . . .
The words ring crystal-clear: "Christ is risen!"
And Christ is risen indeed.

We see the stone rolled from the darkened cavern,
An angel, clothed in white,
Has been sent down from heaven by the Father
To give new hope, new light
To all who sorrow, and our weeping ceases.
We are no longer sad . . .
The greatest news broadcast throughout the ages
Has made us glad.
Christ is risen, the blessed Christ is risen.
Cry it aloud. Oh, emphasize each word!
Lift as one voice a hallelujah chorus
Until the last lone seeking heart has heard.

79

*Christ hath arisen!
O mountain peaks,
attest—witness,
resounding glen
and torrent wave!*

—FELICIA D. HEMANS

Photograph © Marion Brenner/Botanica/Jupiter Images

ON THE THIRD DAY

BILLY GRAHAM

O*n the third day* after His death the Bible says, "And, behold, there was a great earthquake: for the angel of the Lord descended from heaven, and came and rolled back the stone from the door, and sat upon it. His countenance was like lightning, and his raiment white as snow: And for fear of him the keepers did shake, and became as dead men" (Matthew 28:2–4).

Though some Bible students have tried to estimate how much this stone weighed, we need not speculate, because Jesus could have come out of that tomb whether the stone was there or not. The Bible mentions it so that generations to come can know something of the tremendous miracle of Resurrection that took place.

As Mary looked into the tomb she saw "two angels in white sitting, the one at the head, and the other at the feet, where the body of Jesus had lain" (John 20:12). Then one of the angels who was sitting outside the tomb proclaimed the greatest message the world has ever heard: "He is not here: for he is risen" (Matthew 28:6). Those few words changed the history of the universe. Darkness and despair died; hope and anticipation were born in the hearts of men.

80

Cherry tree in bloom in Broesarp, Sweden. Photograph © Sven Halling/PanStock/Jupiter Images

Christ the Lord Is Risen Today

CHARLES WESLEY

TRADITIONAL

1. Christ the Lord is ris'n to-day, Al - le - lu - ia! Sons of men and an - gels say Al - le - lu - ia! Raise your joys and
2. Love's re - deem - ing work is done, Al - le - lu - ia! Fought the fight, the bat - tle won, Al - le - lu - ia! Death in vain for -
3. Lives a - gain our glo - rious King, Al - le - lu - ia! Where, O death, is now thy sting? Al - le - lu - ia! Once He died our

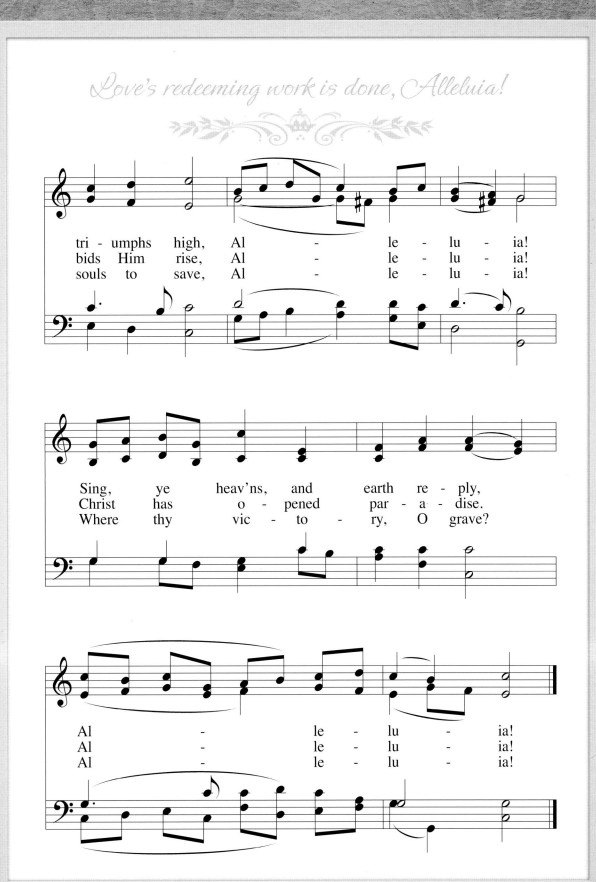

Love's redeeming work is done, Alleluia!

tri - umphs high, Al - le - lu - ia!
bids Him rise, Al - le - lu - ia!
souls to save, Al - le - lu - ia!

Sing, ye heav'ns, and earth re - ply,
Christ has o - pened par - a - dise.
Where thy vic - to - ry, O grave?

Al - le - lu - ia!
Al - le - lu - ia!
Al - le - lu - ia!

Good Morning! Christ Is Risen

Dr. Raphael Harwood Miller

And behold, Jesus met them, saying, "Good morning!" and they came and took hold of His feet and worshiped Him.

So the word was carried to the disciples, "The Lord is risen indeed." And that phrase became the password of the fellowship of the Resurrection. Whenever Christians met one another, the happy greeting was, "The Lord is risen." And the joyous answer came back, "He is risen indeed."

That was the identifying salutation and its appropriate response. It was heard in the crowded streets of Corinth; in the midst of the many-nationed throngs on the temple hill at Jerusalem; among the merchants of Ephesus; from passing ships in the Mediterranean Sea; at the crossways of the desert; and among the servants of Caesar's household.

"Good morning! Christ is risen."

That set men singing at their tasks; it gave meaning to daily living; it opened long vistas of exploration toward the truth; it bought courage to the suffering; it lightened heavy burdens; it sustained the martyr in his ordeal; it gave hope to the oppressed and made faith in spiritual purpose the answer to the unsolved mysteries of the universe.

The night after the crucifixion was the darkest night of the world. Death had held dominion over life until Christ came. The ancient world was haunted by the grave. Human thought and activity were never free from the specter of death's impending and awful finality. Life was lived in a tomb.

Intimations of immortality were but wandering fires that flared and sank to leave the darkness blacker yet. The death of Christ by itself only aggravated the tragedy and deepened the mystery. The most victorious Life the world has ever seen succumbed upon the cruel cross, and the grave enshrouded all His glowing deeds and bright promises.

84

Photograph © Dennis Frates

Nothing could solve that riddle or redeem that tragedy but His Resurrection.

Without Christ's Resurrection, life is a dream without substance, a progress without purpose, and a journey without destination. Before Christ's Resurrection, the thought of eternal life was considered too good to be true; but since the first Easter morning, it is too good *not* to be true. We live in a world where what is good enough can be made true and where faith in the utmost grows from more to more.

"Good morning! Christ is risen."

Every fresh adventure of the human spirit, every new crusade against embattled wrong, every daring excursion across the frontiers of knowledge, every costly devotion to freedom's cause, every undaunted endeavor for a world of peace and good will, every tireless struggle for justice and equality, every heroic martyrdom for faith—all—all go forth under the cloudless Resurrection morning whose sun shall stand still and whose light shall not fail until the work is done.

"Fear not. . . . I am the Living One; and I was dead, and behold, I am alive forevermore and I have the keys. . . ."

"I was dead." And when He died, the world died, with every human hope and every beautiful dream's fulfillment.

"I have the keys." He found His way through the darkest night that ever held the world in the black grip of horror, and He unlocked the tightest tomb ever sealed by human perversity and sin.

And He will find His way and ours through every night and out of every grave.

So we greet one another this Easter Day:

"Good morning! Christ is risen."

And the white-robed and joyous guests of God answer from heavenly places in Christ Jesus.

"He is risen indeed."

Photograph © Ingo Arndt/Minden Pictures

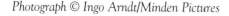

86

The Glorious Dawn

ELLA E. DOXSEE

Gone is the fear that has held us in bondage
As we think of that first Easter Day,
The glorious dawn after earth's darkest night
And the tomb with the stone rolled away.

Angels came down from heaven that day
To roll the great stone from the tomb,
To tell man that Christ lived once again,
And to rob the grave of its fear and its gloom.

The promise of life eternal is ours;
For this we rejoice on this glad Easter Day,
For the Lord of all hath conquered the grave
And the stone has been rolled forever away.

Christ Is Alive!

BEVERLY J. ANDERSON

Rejoice! Rejoice! It's Easter Day;
The angels rolled the stone away.
Christ conquered death and sin and strife
To give to us eternal life.

Triumphantly the church bells ring:
"Christ is alive—our risen King!"
Oh, blessed assurance, saving grace,
One day we'll see Him face to face.

Today the message shines anew,
Its aged promise ever true.
How can a soul be sad, I say;
For hope was born on Easter Day.

Rejoice! Rejoice! Be glad of heart
For all that Easter doth impart.
Christ is alive! Oh, let us sing
Hosannas to our risen King!

Sunrise in Anza Borrego Desert State Park, California.
Photograph © Dennis Frates

THE DAY OF THE RISEN CHRIST

EASTER MORN

Why do you look for the living among the dead? He is not here; he has risen! Remember how he told you, while he was still with you in Galilee: 'The Son of Man must be delivered into the hands of sinful men, be crucified and on the third day be raised again.'" Then they remembered his words.
—LUKE 24:5b–8 (NIV)

Spring bursts today,
for Christ is risen and
all the earth's at play.
—CHRISTINA ROSSETTI

O risen Christ! O Easter flower!
How dear Thy grace has grown!
From east to west, with loving power,
Make all the world Thine own.
—PHILLIPS BROOKS

I am the resurrection,
and the life: he that believeth in me,
though he were dead, yet shall he live:
And whosoever liveth and
believeth in me shall never die.
—JOHN 11:25–26

Ye heavens, how sang they in your courts,
How sang the angelic choir that day,
When from His tomb the imprisoned God,
Like the strong sunrise, broke away?
—REVEREND FREDERICK WILLIAM FABER

Now let the heavens be joyful,
Let Earth her song begin,
Let the round world keep triumph
And all that is therein.
Let all things seen and unseen
Their notes in gladness blend;
For Christ the Lord hath risen,
Our Joy that hath no end!
—JOHN OF DAMASCUS

'Twas Easter Sunday.
The full-blossomed trees filled all
the air with fragrance and with joy.
—HENRY WADSWORTH LONGFELLOW

For I remember it is Easter morn,
And life and love and peace are all new-born.
—ALICE FREEMAN PALMER

Hallelujah! Hallelujah!
On the third morning He arose,
Bright with victory o'er his foes.
Sing we lauding,
And applauding,
Hallelujah!
—JOHN MASON NEALE

91

Easter spells out beauty,
the rare beauty of new life.
—S. D. GORDON

Once more to new creation
Awake, and death gainsay,
For death is swallowed up of life,
And Christ is risen today!
—GEORGE NEWELL LOVEJOY

Well pleaseth me
the sweet time of Easter
that maketh the leaf
and the flower come out.
—BERTRAN DE BORN

In the Morning

CHRIS AHLEMANN

It is in the morning that I see Him
In each dew-drenched daffodil
As I stroll along the silent lane
Then slowly climb the hill.
I climb until I'm near the top,
Where the grass is cool and green,
And here I sit and meditate
On all those things unseen.
A grateful heart, a tranquil breast,
And joy spouting from love
Float to me as on a breeze
From the Father up above.
And when I rise to descend the path
And the sunrise do behold,
I smile to know that I met Him
In the morning, like Mary of old.

93

Sunrise Service

REGINALD HOLMES

I shall worship in my garden
When the grass is wet with dew,
In a special sunrise service
When the Easter skies are blue.
There will be no massive pulpit
And no richly vested choir,
Just an altar built by nature
And a towering maple spire.
There will be no organ playing
With its loud and vibrant notes;
But a hymn of praise will echo
From a hundred songbird throats.
There I'll kneel in supplication
In a setting calm and still
And sip lightly from the chalice
Of a golden daffodil.

Columbines in the San Juan Mountains,
Colorado. Photograph © Marc Muench

THE STORY OF JESUS

CHARLES DICKENS

My dear children, I am very anxious that you should know something about the history of Jesus Christ, for everybody ought to know about Him. No one ever lived who was so good, so kind, so gentle, and so sorry for all people who did wrong, or were in any way ill or miserable, as He was.

That you may know what the people meant when they said "Crucify Him!" I must tell you that in those times, which were very cruel times indeed (let us thank God and Jesus Christ that they are past!), it was the custom to kill people who were sentenced to death by nailing them alive on a great wooden cross planted upright in the ground and leaving them there, exposed to the sun and wind, day and night until they died of pain and thirst. It was the custom, too, to make them walk to the place of execution, carrying the cross-piece of wood to which their hands were to be after-wards nailed; that their shame and suffering might be the greater.

Bearing His Cross upon His shoulder, like the commonest and most wicked crim-inal, our blessed Savior, Jesus Christ, surrounded by the persecuting crowd, went out of Jerusalem to a place called, in the Hebrew language, Golgotha—that is, the place of a skull. And, having come to a hill called Mount Calvary, they hammered cruel nails through His hands and feet and nailed Him on the cross between two other crosses, on each of which a common thief was nailed in agony. Over His head, they fastened this writing: "Jesus of Nazareth, the King of the Jews" in three languages— Hebrew, Greek, and Latin.

At about the sixth hour, a deep and terrible darkness came over all the land and lasted until the ninth hour, when Jesus cried out with a loud voice, "My God, My God, why hast Thou forsaken Me!" The soldiers, hearing Him, dipped a sponge in some vinegar that was standing there and, fastening it to a long reed, put it up to His mouth. When He had received it, He said "It is finished!" And crying "Father! Into Thy hands I commend My Spirit!" He died. . . .

The next day being the Sabbath, the Jews were anxious that the bodies should be taken down at once and made that request to Pilate. Therefore some soldiers came and

94

THE GLORY OF EASTER

Bald Knob Cross in Alto Pass, Illinois. Photograph © Jason Lindsey/Perceptive Visions Stock Photography

broke the legs of the two criminals to kill them; but coming to Jesus and finding Him already dead, they only pierced His side with a spear. From the wound there came out blood and water.

There was a good man named Joseph of Arimathea, a Jewish City, who believed in Christ, and going to Pilate privately (for fear of the Jews) begged that he might have the body. Pilate consenting, he and one Nicodemus rolled it in linen and spices, because it was the custom of the Jews to prepare bodies for burial in that way; then they buried it in a new tomb or sepulcher, which had been cut out of a rock in a garden near the place of crucifixion, and where no one had ever yet been buried. They then rolled a great stone to the mouth of the sepulcher and left Mary Magdalene and the other Mary, sitting there, watching it.

The chief priests and Pharisees, remembering that Jesus Christ had said to His disciples that He would rise from the grave on the third day after His death, went to Pilate and prayed that the sepulcher might be well taken care of until that day, lest the disciples should steal the body and afterwards say to the people that Christ was risen from the dead. Since Pilate agreed to this, a guard of soldiers was set over it constantly, and the stone was sealed up besides. And so it remained, watched and sealed, until the third day, which was the first day of the week.

When that morning began to dawn, Mary Magdalene and the other Mary and some other women came to the sepulcher with some more spices which they had prepared. As they were saying to each other, "How shall we roll away the stone?" the earth trembled and shook, and an angel, descending from heaven, rolled it back and then sat resting on it. His countenance was like lightning, and his garments were white as snow; at sight of him, the men of the guard fainted away with fear, as if they were dead.

Mary Magdalene saw the stone rolled away, ran to Peter and John, who were coming towards the place, and said, "They have taken away the Lord and we know not where they have laid Him!" They immediately ran to the tomb. When Peter came up, he went in and saw the linen clothes lying in one place and a napkin that had been bound about the head in another. John also went in then and saw the same things. Then they went home to tell the rest.

But Mary Magdalene remained outside the sepulcher, weeping. After a little time, she stooped down and looked in and saw two angels, clothed in white, sitting where the body of Christ had lain. These said to her, "Woman, why weepest Thou?" She answered, "Because they have taken away my Lord, and I know not where they have laid Him."

As she gave this answer, she turned round and saw Jesus standing behind her but did not then know Him. "Woman," said He, "Why weepest Thou? What seekest thou?" She, supposing Him to be the gardener, replied, "Sir! If Thou hast borne my Lord hence, tell me where

Thou hast laid Him, and I will take Him away." Jesus pronounced her name, "Mary." Then she knew Him and, starting, exclaimed "Master!"

"Touch me not," said Christ; "for I am not yet ascended to My father; but go to My disciples, and say unto them, I ascend unto My Father, and your Father, and to My God, and to your God!"

Accordingly, Mary Magdalene went and told the disciples that she had seen Christ, and what He had said to her; and with them she found the other women whom she had left at the sepulcher when she had gone to call those two disciples, Peter and John. These women told her and the rest that they had seen at the tomb two men in shining garments, at sight of whom they had been afraid and had bent down, but who had told them that the Lord was risen; and also that as they came to tell this, they had seen Christ on the way and had held Him by the feet and worshipped Him. But these accounts seemed to the apostles at that time as idle tales, and they did not believe them.

The soldiers of the guard, too, when they recovered from their fainting fit and went to the chief priests to tell them what they had seen, were silenced with large sums of money and were told by them to say that the disciples had stolen the body away while they were asleep.

But it happened that on that same day, Simon and Cleopas—Simon, one of the twelve apostles, and Cleopas, one of the followers of Christ—were walking to a village called

Emmaus, at some little distance from Jerusalem, and were talking by the way upon the death and Resurrection of Christ. They were joined by a stranger who explained the Scriptures to them and told them a great deal about God, so that they wondered at His knowledge. As the night was fast coming on when they reached the village, they asked this stranger to stay with them, which He consented to do. When they all three sat down to supper, He took some bread, blessed it, and broke it—as Christ had done at the Last Supper. Looking on Him in wonder, they found that His face was changed before them and that it was Christ Himself; and as they looked on Him, He disappeared.

They instantly rose up and returned to Jerusalem, and, finding the disciples sitting together, told them what they had seen. While they were speaking, Jesus suddenly stood in the midst of all the company and said, "Peace be unto you!" Seeing that they were greatly frightened, He showed them His hands and feet and invited them to touch Him. . . .

But Thomas, one of the twelve apostles, was not there at that time; and when the rest said to him afterwards, "We have seen the Lord!" he answered, "Except I shall see in His hands the print of the nails, and thrust my hand into His side, I will not believe!" At that moment, though the doors were all shut, Jesus again appeared, standing among them, and said, "Peace be unto you!" Then He said to Thomas, "Reach hither thy finger, and behold My hands;

and reach hither thy hand, and thrust it into My side; and be not faithless, but believing."

And Thomas answered, and said to Him, "My Lord and my God!" Then said Jesus, "Thomas, because thou hast seen Me, thou hast believed. Blessed are they that have not seen Me, and yet have believed."

After that time, Jesus Christ was seen by five hundred of His followers at once, and He remained with others of them forty days, teaching them, and instructing them to go forth into the world and preach His gospel and religion, not minding what wicked men might do to them. And conducting His disciples at last out of Jerusalem as far as Bethany, He blessed them and ascended in a cloud to heaven and took His place at the right hand of God. And while they gazed into the bright blue sky where He had vanished, two white-robed angels appeared among them and told them that as they had seen Christ ascend to heaven, so He would, one day, come descending from it to judge the world.

When Christ was seen no more, the apostles began to teach the people as He had commanded them. And through the power He had given them, they healed the sick and gave sight to the blind, speech to the dumb, and hearing to the deaf as He had done. They took the name of Christians from our Savior Christ.

Fellowship and Celebration

Chapter Four

Tranquility
ABIGAIL FALK

While the earth is swathed in darkness
And stars still mask the sky,
Our vision catches a dim light
That day is drawing nigh.
Amid the reverent hush of dawn
And scented springtime air,
The glory of Easter morning
Is with us everywhere.

Just as the lovely flowers unfold
Petals of every hue,
Inspired by the plan divine
To start a life anew,
Our hearts fill with the surge of joy
Of newfound hope that in
The Resurrection of our Lord
New life we may begin.

We find in this brief morning hour
Tranquility to lift
Our spirits with the boundlessness
Of God's great Easter gift.
Our hearts sing out again for joy,
Our thankfulness we voice.
The song of triumph now proclaim,
Christ is risen—Rejoice! Rejoice!

Easter Sunrise
DONITA M. DYER

An hour before the sun did rise
That morning long ago,
Christ rose in glorious triumph,
For God ordained it so.

He spoke to Mary at the tomb
Before He went away
To prove the sweet reality
Of that first Easter day!

The dim light of the breaking dawn
Reflected on His face
And turned that shadowy garden
Into a lovely place.

And still today, on Easter Morn,
Though centuries have gone by,
We reverently bow in worship
And lift hearts to sanctify.

In awe we watch the sun's gold beams
As they glide into view,
For they tint the veiled horizon
In rich, resplendent hue.

The sun now shines as if inspired,
In just the same bright way
That it reflected His dear face
On that glad Easter Day.

100

*Cades Cove in Great Smoky Mountains National Park,
Tennessee. Photograph © Terry Donnelly/Austin Donnelly*

EASTER CELEBRATIONS

LANSING CHRISTMAN

I never fail to participate in two Easter Sunday services: one in the out-of-doors and another in the country church. For the service at sunrise, I go to the sanctuary of the hills. There I look and listen, absorbing all I can of nature and spring as I ponder the greatness of the universe.

I celebrate the promise of eternal life as the rays of the morning sun rise above the eastern horizon. The rebirth and renewal are so evident in what I see and hear. I behold God's gift of sun and song, bulb and bloom, of stirring seed and sprout.

103

After the sunrise ritual, I go to the old country church nestled in the foothills of the Blue Ridge Mountains. Spring has graced the landscape with the splendor of peach-tree blossoms.

The Gothic architecture of the church, based on churches built centuries ago in Western Europe, is an imposing array of ribbed vaulting, pointed arches, flying buttresses, steep roofs, and a lofty steeple pointing to the heavens above. Its beauty is majestic to behold.

The stained-glass windows of the sanctuary portray the major events in the ministry of Christ. As I listen to the hymns of praise and the messages of Easter, I continue my celebration of the Resurrection. This glorious day, my spiritual needs are satisfied. There is the promise, the reassurance of life without end.

View of Mount Washington from Sugar Hill, New Hampshire.
Photograph © William H. Johnson

The Bells of Easter
Dolores Cains

Easter bells ring out at dawn
Their message o'er the way.
They tell us of the risen Christ
Who dwells in us today.

As sunlight floods the valley
And tips the trees with gold,
Their joyful music fills the air
As Easter's tale is told.

The melodies of love and hope
Peal out so sweet and clear
And bring a quiet peacefulness
To all of those who hear.

And when the tunes are ended
And the last note fades away,
We find our hearts uplifted
On this glad Easter Day.

104

Easter
Hattie Pope

There's a glow on Easter morning
In rose-tinted eastern sky.
There is dew upon the lilies;
Church bells ring from belfries high,
Ringing clear in perfect rhythm
In the cool, fresh morning air,
Calling all to join and worship
In a Resurrection prayer.

There is joy on Easter morning
When we hear the Gospel read,
Telling Jesus Christ our Savior
Has arisen from the dead.
Oh, with prayerful hearts uplifted,
We should all join in to sing,
"Christ is risen, hallelujah,
And He lives, our Lord and King."

Easter Bells
Cleo King

Ring the bells of Easter,
Ring them out once more.
Let them tell the story
They have told before.

Let them greet the sunrise
Of this Easter Day
With the glad announcement:
The stone is rolled away.

Let their notes of triumph
At this joyful time
Sound the Resurrection
In each golden chime.

Then may hope and gladness
Come to every heart
As we catch the message
Easter bells impart.

Christ Lutheran Church, Plattsmouth, Nebraska. Photograph
© Grant Heilman/Grant Heilman Photography

Easter Joy

MERLE MARQUIS FRANK

Let children's happy voices sing
And glad exultant church bells ring.
Let flowers waft perfume on high
And people's praises rend the sky.
For hope has sprung from empty tomb
Which sealed for sin and death their doom;
And man, estranged from God, restored
Because He bore our sins, my Lord.
A fruitful life He offered me
When He made death so glorious be.
His love, His work, His power, His way
He gave on Resurrection day.

106

Easter Prayer

KAY HOFFMAN

Once again it's Easter morning,
And joyous church bells ring.
"Christ, our Lord, is risen!"
The white-robed choirs sing.

The Easter message is retold
As it has been before—
How the angels rolled away the stone
From the tomb's dark door.

Our hearts are joined in one accord
As now we humbly pray:
"From our heart's door this Easter morn,
Lord, roll the stone away."

*Iris blooms along Metolius River, in Deschutes National
Forest, Oregon. Photograph © age fotostock/SuperStock*

A Different Celebration

Alma Barkman

The young minister had challenged us to celebrate Easter a little differently, and so, very early in the morning on the first day of the week, I found myself driving to church in the predawn darkness with two quarts of milk, a dozen eggs, and three bags of pancake mix. I confess, I wondered a little about those early Christians whom we were supposed to be emulating. Had they also marked the occasion of Easter by gathering together for breakfast?

Maybe they too had been so busy mixing the pancake batter that the sun burst forth upon them before they were really ready for the day. Tossing aside my apron, I hurried out of the church kitchen to join the sunrise celebration. The Peters and Jameses and Andrews of our small congregation were already gathered on the lawn of our little suburban church. I quietly tiptoed out to join the circle of believers, my footsteps crushing icy crystals in the grass.

With no musical accompaniment, we began to sing, "Jesus lives! Thy terrors now can no longer, Death, appall us. . . ." Our voices sounded weak and unsteady. Perhaps it was the latent moisture oozing into my shoes that was giving me cold feet, but I was sure these old Easter hymns must sound like idle squawking to disbelieving neighbors on either side of the church. Why, even a nearby crow was poking fun at our voices. Or, as the young minister suggested, perhaps the crow really had been sent to help us make a "joyful noise unto the Lord." With my face warming to the sun, my soul was rising to the message: "Jesus lives! Our hearts know well naught from us His love shall sever. . . ."

The sunshine was glinting off the puddles in the unpaved parking lot as we scraped the mud from our shoes and reentered the church. The kitchen was no longer dark and gloomy, but a warm, inviting haven filled with friends and fellowship and the tantalizing smell of fresh coffee. Somehow, I think even the apostles would have appreciated my pancakes.

Exterior of Saint Benedict's Catholic Church, Honaunau,
Hawaii Islands. Photograph © Glow Images/SuperStock

109

Easter Thoughts

KATHLEEN LEMMON

I want to worship in God's house
This holy Sabbath day.
I want to hear the Scripture read,
To sing and softly pray.

The message of the Easter morn
Will fill my heart again.
"He lives, my Savior lives in me"
Will be the glad refrain.

The Valley Church

ELMA ROWBOTHAM

The valley church is yours and mine;
It has an open door.
Green-robed mountains are the walls
And valley grass its floor.
The roof is but a sweep of sky
Illumined by the sun
Or, when night shades the vale, the stars,
Appearing one and one.
The altar is a dogwood tree;
We kneel before such grace.
An altar cloth so chaste and white
The lilies at its base.
The valley church has sanctity,
For here have angels trod.
Here we may worship and behold
The presence of our God.

The Little Town Church

LOISE PINKERTON FRITZ

Springtime has come to the little town church,
The little town church of white.
The spreading, lone forsythia
Is covered with florets bright,
Beautiful florets of yellowish-gold
That brighten the still-dull earth.
Springtime has come in a colorful dress,
And come to this small-town church.

Easter has come to the little town church,
The little town church I know.
The choir is singing "Christ's risen today,"
While bells chime sounds of hope.
Easter has come to the little town church,
To churches in cities and dells.
And the Christ of Easter shall come and dwell
In the hearts of the people as well.

*First Church of Christ (Congregational) in Clinton,
Connecticut. Photograph © William H. Johnson*

Light the Candles

GRACE NOLL CROWELL

Light the candles, set the tall white lilies
High upon the altar of your heart.
Place the picture of the newly-risen
Christ above that altar—set apart
This day for worship and for glad rejoicing,
For once, before the dawn, the Christ arose,
And hope that had been crushed to earth sprang upward
More radiant than any light that glows.

Hold fast that hope, keep faith's white fire burning.
Cling close to truth, and it will make you free.
Doubt not that He who had been dead is risen
To be our light throughout eternity.
"Because I live," He said, "ye shall live also."
Cry out the news to hearts that grope in need.
Let the glad tidings be your Easter greeting:
"The Christ is risen, the Christ is risen indeed!"

On an Easter Morn

JESSIE CANNON ELDRIDGE

Let me think deeply when the Easter comes,
Look to my soul and weigh its faith and hope,
Rededicate it; then lead those who grope
In unbelief into the light that sums
Our living up in such a wondrous way;
Show them the meaning of the Easter songs,
The lily flowers, the gathering of the throngs,
The hallelujahs; teach them how to pray.
We should be happy on an Easter morn,
Rejoicing with Christ's glorious rebirth,
Joining to spread His message around the earth
And beckoning others to again be born.

Call all who wander, who have sinned, known loss,
"Come, rise again, and conquer o'er the cross!"

Easter

MONA K. GULDSWOG

I saw Easter in the eyes of one small child;
Wonder was there, a breathless moment
When trust in God shone purely
As slim white tapers upon an altar
    of innocence.

I saw Easter in a mother's gentle smile;
Joy was there, the glory of His Resurrection
Setting hope to sing within her heart,
An echo to the ringing steeple bells.

I saw Easter in the hands of one old man;
Faith was there, gnarled and wrinkled,
Yet they formed a silent prayer,
To each sacred word a reverent Amen.

May Easter be mirrored across the land,
In countless hearts a holy flame,
Abiding in wonder, joy, and faith,
An alleluia to His name.

113

O Sons and Daughters, Let Us Sing

Jean Tisserand,
translated by John M. Neale

Traditional French

Al - le - lu - ia! Al - le - lu - ia!

Al - le - lu - ia! Al - le - lu - ia!

1. O sons and daugh - ters, let us sing! The
2. That night the a - pos - tles met in fear; A -
3. On this most ho - ly day of days, To

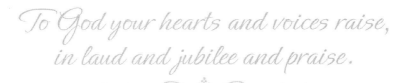

Easter Morning
EVELYN WEEKS TAYLOR

Easter Morning! Easter Morning!
Cherub choirs sweetly sing.
Little faces scrubbed and shining,
"Christ is risen!" their voices ring.

Little chapels, widely scattered,
Great cathedrals, spires so tall—
Yet the echo, "Christ is Risen!"
Rises skyward from them all.

The Choir
ALBERTA DODSON

Young folks, side by side,
Seated row on row,
Welcome Eastertide
With a hallowed glow.

Reverently their flush
Heralds springtime joys;
Hallelujahs rise
To make a joyful noise.

Harbingers of spring,
They are here to share.
Roseate, they sing
Easter's joyous prayer.

Country church near Wonalancet, New Hampshire. Photograph © William H. Johnson

SINGING A NEW SONG

PAMELA KENNEDY

he choir director cut us off after the chorus . . . again. She sighed and stared at her music for a moment, then looked up and said, "Okay, let's take a ten-minute break. Get some water, walk around, get some fresh air, then come back and let's try this one more time."

We could sense her discouragement. To be truthful, we were all discouraged. The church choir contained about twenty folks of varying ages, talents, and devotion to music. Some were in the "make a joyful noise" category. A few had some professional training. Most of us just enjoyed singing. It was early April, and Easter was bearing down on us like a runaway locomotive. The closer it came, the more we felt there was going to be a terrible train wreck!

The tenors couldn't get their harmony line together. The altos overwhelmed the other sections with both enthusiasm and volume. There were some uncontrolled trillers among the sopranos, and the bassos fluctuated between booming and absolute silence. With just a week to go, panic was setting in.

We regrouped after the break, freshly determined to get our alleluias organized and on-key. The director raised her arms, nodded to the organist, and we began. We made it through a difficult modulation with success, and the choir director smiled a bit. The bassos held down their *profundos* and the shy tenors gained enough courage to attack their harmony line with solidarity. Then came the *a cappella* section. We sang with enthusiasm, every note increasing in volume and intensity, enunciating with clarity, ending on one strong, unison note. Then the organ echoed our voices with a triumphant chord— and revealed we were a full tone flat. The director's face reddened with frustration at the echoing dissonance. "Well, that could wake the dead!" she announced.

Initially tempted to suggest that was an appropriate response for an Easter piece, I quickly thought better of it.

Frustration stalked the next few rehearsals. We conquered one part, only to mess up

A stained glass window in the National Cathedral in Washington, D.C.
Photograph © Brian Meeks/iStockphoto.com

on another. This was supposed to be done to the glory of God—would He be embarrassed? Would we? Not many of us were optimistic.

Easter morning was gray, and the air smelled more like winter than spring. As the organ played the prelude, we filed into our places in the choir loft. The pastor offered his morning prayer. We raised our books in unison and opened them, focusing on the director as she raised her arms. Then we sang. Parts that had never been quite right intertwined beautifully. Each section seemed inspired by the others. We were together, a choir in the truest sense, and, when we hit the final note, the music hung in the air for a moment, floating over the congregation like an offering. In the end, at the final hour, it all came together.

I suspect our musical experience is not really unique. All across the country choirs struggle through compositions that seem impossible, under directors who must feel they should have chosen another calling. But in the end, when their efforts are offered up, God makes something beautiful of the anticipated failure. And isn't that what Easter is all about? After the disaster of Good Friday, the despair of a Sabbath in the tomb, who would have expected a new song of triumph? But the fear and failure experienced only days earlier turned to joy and thanksgiving through the mercy of a loving God. The offering was accepted, the prayer answered.

Not just at Easter, but also all through the year, whenever we sing a new song for the Lord, whenever we proclaim His salvation and give Him praise, He takes our imperfections and failures and produces beauty. As He has been, He continues to be: a God of Resurrection.

Garden in Mt. Angel, Oregon. Photograph © Steve Terrill

EASTER FELLOWSHIP

But if we walk in the light, as he is in the light, we have fellowship one with another, and the blood of Jesus Christ his Son cleanseth us from all sin.
—1 JOHN 1:7 (NIV)

May hope dwell warmly in your heart
While all the world rejoices.
Now sing His praises sweet and clear
With true and grateful voices.
—BRIAN F. KING

Heaven and earth,
and saints and friends and
flowers are keeping Easter Day!
—AUTHOR UNKNOWN

Once more an Easter morning
Has dawned this blessed day
To tell the world our Savior rose—
The stone was rolled away.
For truth has triumphed over wrong,
And nature's best display
Joins with God's followers to share
The joy of Easter Day.
—CARICE WILLIAMS

Father, thank You for the truth
of Your Resurrection and the
celebrations with other believers
that make it all the more meaningful.
—ALMA BARKMAN

Oh, Easter anthems gladly sing,
Let all the bells form towers ring,
And sun dispel with brightening rays
The darkness of the Passion days!
—JOSEPHINE RICE CREELMAN

Ye sleeping buds, break
Open your green cerements, and wake
To fragrant blossoming for His sweet sake.
—MARGARET FRENCH PATTO

I think of the garden after the rain,
And hope to my heart comes singing.
At morn the cherry blooms will be white,
And the Easter bells be ringing!
—EDNA D. PROCTOR

May the Easter sunrise chase every cloud away,
Bringing many blessings and joy to fill your day.
—PEARL MCKINNEY

Let all the jubilant sounds of earth
swing up in one resonant wave of
triumphant song. Let us robe ourselves
in the sunny gladness of a hope so bright—
the hope that defies death . . .
—ISAAC MASSEY HALDEMAN

Tulips marching, two by two,
On stately stems in brilliant hue.
Children marching, two by four,
Marching through the front church door,
Dressed in tulips' brilliant hues
To brighten somber, stately pews.
—KATHRYN STEPHENSON WILHELM

123

It is the hour to rend thy chains,
The blossom time of souls.
—KATHERINE LEE BATES

Easter Bouquet

BEVERLY J. ANDERSON

A vision of spring passed my way
In form of an Eastertime bouquet—
Forget-me-nots of powder blue,
Roses sweet of every hue,
Daffodils of sunny gold,
All so lovely to behold.
Lavender lilacs, daisies of white,
Tulips too in colors bright,
Pink sweet peas, and pansies gay—
All on parade this Easter Day.
From childhood's garden of flowers and lace
And an angel smile upon each face—
Joyful, frilly little girls
With shining eyes and golden curls
Form an Eastertime bouquet,
Dressed in Sunday-school array.

Easter Morn

GEORGIA B. ADAMS

See them lined up in a row
Here in church on Easter morn,
Sitting in the family pew
From oldest boy to one just born,

Mom and Dad at either end.
See them dressed so trim and neat—
Girls beribboned, boys with ties
As so quietly they meet.

Sunday mornings year around
See them fill the family pew,
Families all together praying—
Mother, Dad, and children too.

Lupine on Steptoe Butte in Whitman County, Washington.
Photograph by Mary Liz Austin/Austin Donnelly Photography

The Road to Emmaus

Luke 24:13-48

And, behold, two of them went that same day to a village called Emmaus, which was from Jerusalem about threescore furlongs. And they talked together of all these things which had happened.

And it came to pass, that, while they communed together and reasoned, Jesus himself drew near, and went with them. But their eyes were holden that they should not know him.

And he said unto them, What manner of communications are these that ye have one to another, as ye walk, and are sad?

And the one of them, whose name was Cleopas, answering said unto him, Art thou only a stranger in Jerusalem, and hast not known the things which are come to pass there in these days?

And he said unto them, What things? And they said unto him, Concerning Jesus of Nazareth, which was a prophet mighty in deed and word before God and all the people: And how the chief priests and our rulers delivered him to be condemned to death, and have crucified him. But we trusted that it had been he which should have redeemed Israel: and beside all this, to day is the third day since these things were done. Yea, and certain women also of our company made us astonished, which were early at the sepulchre; And when they found not his body, they came, saying, that they had also seen a vision of angels, which said that he was alive. And certain of them which were with us went to the sepulchre, and found it even so as the women had said: but him they saw not.

Then he said unto them, O fools, and slow of heart to believe all that the prophets have spoken: Ought not Christ to have suffered these things, and to enter into his glory? And beginning at Moses and all the prophets, he expounded unto them in all the scriptures the things concerning himself.

And they drew nigh unto the village, whither they went: and he made as though he would have gone further. But they constrained him, saying, Abide with us: for it is toward evening, and the day is far spent. And he went in to tarry with them. And it came to pass, as he sat at meat with them, he took bread, and blessed it, and brake, and gave to them.

And their eyes were opened, and they knew him; and he vanished out of their sight.

And they said one to another, Did not our heart burn within us, while he talked with us by the way, and while he opened to us the scriptures?

And they rose up the same hour, and returned to Jerusalem, and found the eleven gathered together, and them that were with

THE PILGRIMS AT EMMAUS *by Titian. Image* © *Erich Lessing/Art Resource, NY*

them, Saying, The Lord is risen indeed, and hath appeared to Simon. And they told what things were done in the way, and how he was known of them in breaking of bread.

And as they thus spake, Jesus himself stood in the midst of them, and saith unto them, Peace be unto you. But they were terrified and affrighted, and supposed that they had seen a spirit. And he said unto them, Why are ye troubled? and why do thoughts arise in your hearts? Behold my hands and my feet, that it is I myself: handle me, and see; for a spirit hath not flesh and bones, as ye see me have. And when he had thus spoken, he shewed them his hands and his feet.

And while they yet believed not for joy, and wondered, he said unto them, Have ye here any meat? And they gave him a piece of a broiled fish, and of an honeycomb. And he took it, and did eat before them.

And he said unto them, These are the words which I spake unto you, while I was yet with you, that all things must be fulfilled, which were written in the law of Moses, and in the prophets, and in the psalms, concerning me.

Then opened he their understanding, that they might understand the scriptures, And said unto them, Thus it is written, and thus it behooved Christ to suffer, and to rise from the dead the third day: And that repentance and remission of sins should be preached in his name among all nations, beginning at Jerusalem. And ye are witnesses of these things.

RECONCILIATION

NANCY GUTHRIE

Unpaid debts, unmet expectations, and unfinished business finally came to a head for my friends—two couples who were estranged from each other after a business venture hit hard times. Feelings were hurt and the friendship was fractured. They met to work it through, but their attempt seemed to only bring more issues to the surface. Then they found themselves standing at my son Gabe's grave after everyone else had gone, and the four of them embraced. In the sobering reality of that moment, resentment gave way to reconciliation. I've always seen it as a beautiful benediction to Gabe's life, and a blossom of hope growing out of his death.

Reconciliation is close to the heart of God. His desire for reconciliation with those He loves cost Him the ultimate price—His Son. The cross made it possible for you and me to be friends with God. Not merely His servants, but His friends!

Have you been thinking God is mad at you, that He sent difficulties into your life out of anger or retribution for your offenses against Him or apathy toward Him? God is not mad at you. In fact, He has gone to incredible lengths to restore His friendship with you. He did not wait for you to warm up to Him, but in fact, while you were still His enemy, He paid the price of reconciliation with His life. He has taken the first costly step toward you. Won't you take a step toward Him and respond to His offer—not just of salvation but also of friendship?

The cross is the means by which we reconcile not only with God but also with each other. "Together as one body, Christ reconciled both groups to God by means of His death, and our hostility toward each other was put to death" (EPHESIANS 2:16). When we're standing at the foot of the cross, our disagreements and disappointments with each other don't seem to matter so much. And as we gaze on Innocence upon the cross, we simply cannot hold on to the offenses we've built into walls. Now we can enjoy the depth and joy of friendship with each other that reflects our friendship with God. ⊂⊃

129

Cougar Creek in Gifford Pinchot National Forest, Washington. Photograph © Mary Liz Austin/Austin Donnelly Photography

THE Greatest BLESSING

CHAPTER FIVE

Borrowed

AUTHOR UNKNOWN

They borrowed a bed to lay His head
When Christ the Lord came down.
They borrowed a foal in the mountain pass
For Him to ride to town.
But the crown that He wore
And the cross that He bore
    Were His own.

He borrowed the bread when the crowd He fed
On the grassy mountainside;
He borrowed the dish of broken fish
With which He satisfied.
But the crown that He wore
And the cross that He bore
    Were His own.

He borrowed the ship in which to sit
To teach the multitude.
He borrowed the nest in which to rest,
He had never a home as rude.

But the crown that He wore
And the cross that He bore
    Were His own.

He borrowed a room on the way to the tomb,
The Passover lamb to eat.
They borrowed a cave, for Him a grave;
They borrowed a winding sheet.
But the crown that He wore
And the cross that He bore
    Were His own.

The thorns on His head were worn in my stead;
For me the Savior died.
For guilt of my sin the nails drove in
When Him they crucified.
Though the crown that He wore
And the cross that He bore
    Were His own . . .
They rightly were mine, instead.

133

*Christ took our nature on Him,
not that He 'bove all things lov'd it,
for the purity: no, but He drest Him
with our human trim, because our flesh
stood most in need of Him.*

—ROBERT HERRICK

Photograph © Steve Terrill

FREED BY FORGIVENESS

PAMELA KENNEDY

Daily we are offered opportunities to participate in the miracle of forgiveness and the new life it brings. A husband or wife is unkind, forgets a request, or thoughtlessly hurts our feelings. We can choose to bear a grudge or to forgive. A friend repeats gossip about us, takes credit for something we accomplished, or rebuffs us. We can devise ways to get even or release our hurt through the act of forgiving. A child rejects our advice or makes a choice of which we disapprove. We can decide to offer condemnation or to offer forgiveness.

"But they don't even ask for forgiveness! They don't even seem sorry!" we might respond. But when we look at Jesus on the cross, we see that forgiveness is not based on the behavior of the one committing the offense, but rather upon the character of the one who forgives. What a revelation for many of us! We have the power to forgive regardless of what another person chooses to think or do. By forgiving we do not absolve the other person of responsibility; we simply refuse to carry the burden of anger, hatred, or bitterness around any longer. We are freed from the bondage of negative and destructive emotions as well as from the temptation to indulge in bad behavior by getting even or striking back.

At the cross, Jesus demonstrated the cost of God's forgiveness. It required His death. But three days later, He also demonstrated the power of such forgiveness: the freedom of Resurrection and new life. Why should we practice this Easter kind of forgiveness? I believe the key is found several places in the Scripture, but perhaps it is stated most clearly in the two verses immediately following what we refer to as the Lord's Prayer: "For if you forgive men when they sin against you, your heavenly Father will also forgive you. But if you do not forgive men their sins, your Father will not forgive your sins" (MATTHEW 6:14, 15 NIV). Our ability to receive God's forgiveness is inextricably bound up in our own willingness to extend it to others. If we harbor an unforgiving spirit, we only hurt ourselves.

Forgiveness is not a sign of weakness, but of strength. It makes us partners in the great compassion that God extended to mankind at Calvary two thousand years ago.

134

Middle North Falls in Silver Falls State Park, Oregon. Photograph © Mary Liz Austin/Austin Donnelly Photography

If Jesus could look upon those who brutalized and berated Him and offer them forgiveness, can we do less to those who hurt us? Forgiveness is an opportunity to experience the freeing power of the Resurrection every day. It is often difficult, but we can take comfort in the knowledge that God does not ask us to do anything He does not empower us to accomplish.

THE GREATEST BLESSING

In the Garden

C. Austin Miles

1. I come to the gar - den a - lone while the
2. He speaks, and the sound of His voice is so
3. I'd stay in the gar - den with Him though the

dew is still on the ros - es, and the
sweet the birds hush their sing - ing, and the
night a - round me be fall - ing, but He

voice I hear fall - ing on my ear, the
mel - o - dy that He gave to me with -
bids me go; thro' the voice of woe His

Son of God dis - clos - es.
in my heart is ring - ing.
voice to me is call - ing.

The sound of His voice is so sweet the
birds hush their singing . . .

And He walks with me, and He talks with me, and He

tells me I am His own; and the

joy we share as we tar - ry there, none

oth - er has ev - er known.

He Passed This Way

LETITIA MORSE NASH

He passed this way, and sleeping earth
Springs to life beneath His feet;
The seeds and bulbs that dormant lay
Send forth a message, green and sweet.
The hard, bare trees that for long months
Gave not a sign of growth or life
Burst into leaf and blossom fair,
And all the earth with joy is rife.
Tall Easter lilies, white and fair,
Proclaim the triumph of our King.
He passed this way, and all the earth
Shall joyously His praises sing.

He passed this way, and stumbling feet
Walk straight and sure because He came.
And hands that faltered at their task
Are blessed and strengthened in His name.
He makes the groping blind to see,
The deaf to hear, the dumb to speak,
And brings a blessing of sweet peace
To troubled ones that comfort seek.
He heals the broken hearts of men
And does their haunting fears allay.
And earth may hope this Eastertime
Because our Savior passed this way.

138

Garden with flowering bougainvillea at the Thyme Garden in Alsea, Oregon. Photograph © Dennis Frates

UNENDING JOURNEY

KEN DUNCAN

*O*ne *Sunday morning,* centuries ago, a vacancy sign went up outside a tomb in Jerusalem. That never happens—in Jerusalem or anywhere. Tombs are empty or full—never vacant. That would mean that someone had occupied the space and then had vacated it. Dead people don't vacate.

Jesus did.

But not because He was dead. First, He left death and then the grave behind. He arose! He was seen walking, talking, and eating. Those who had seen His hands and feet nailed to the cross thought it was over, that Jesus would never walk again. His death confirmed their fears. But they had forgotten He had foreseen their confusion and had encouraged them to be patient. They only had to wait three days.

These early followers were too afraid to wait—too ashamed to wait—too devastated to wait. So they were surprised! And they went from being stunned by His death to being overwhelmed by His Resurrection. They were changed.

Jesus rose bodily. That means, among other things, that He had more walking to do, more steps to take. The promise of the Resurrection includes this amazing thought: we will spend eternity walking where Jesus walked. And He will walk with us. ✺

The tomb of Lazarus, cut into the rock in Bethany, south of Jerusalem, Israel. Photograph © Erich Lessing/Art Resource, NY

Always Easter

GRACE V. WATKINS

You say it happened long ago
And in a far-off land
Where men and women spoke a tongue
I would not understand,
That centuries have come and gone
Since that triumphant day,
And that the garden where He walked
Is half a world away.

He walks in every garden, friend;
And every rock-sealed tomb
Opens 'neath His shining hand
As springtime flowers bloom.
For every dawn is Easter dawn:
On every sunrise hill
The earthbound glimpse eternity
And meet the Master still.

143

With thankful hearts we sing our joyous alleluiahs to Christ, our risen King!

—MABEL CLARE THOMAS

Photograph © Jon Gnass

MEANING AND INFLUENCE

So now we can rejoice in our wonderful new relationship with God because our Lord Jesus Christ has made us friends of God.
—ROMANS 5:11 (NLT)

*C*ome, ye saints, look here and wonder,
See the place where Jesus lay;
He has burst His bands asunder;
He has borne our sins away;
Joyful tidings,
Yes, the Lord has risen today.
—THOMAS KELLY

May you rejoice
in the gladness
of this Easter season,
And may the message
of new life and hope
remain with you always!
—PEARL McKINNEY

Keep watch over yourselves
and all the flock of which the Holy
Spirit has made you overseers.
Be shepherds of the church of God,
which he bought with his own blood.
—ACTS 20:28 (NIV)

Rise, heart! thy Lord is risen. Sing His praise
Without delays.
Who takes thee by the hand, that thou likewise
With Him mayst rise—
That as His death condemned thee to dust,
His life may make thee gold; and much more just.

—GEORGE HERBERT

Easter is the demonstration
of God that life is essentially
spiritual and timeless.

—CHARLES M. CROWE

The Resurrection gives my life
meaning and direction and the opportunity
to start over no matter what my circumstances.

—ROBERT FLATT

The event of the Resurrection
brought a new perspective to the
vision of man. No longer was he
restricted to the little distance of
an earthly existence. The horizon
melted away, as it were, and he
could glimpse beyond the clouds
the golden glory of eternal life.

—ESTHER YORK BURKHOLDER

Let every man and woman
count himself immortal.
Let him catch the revelation
of Jesus in His Resurrection.
Let him say not merely,
"Christ is risen," but "I shall rise."

—PHILLIPS BROOKS

*On Easter Day the veil between
time and eternity thins to gossamer.*

—DOUGLAS HORTON

Grace Incarnate

ENID MARTELL OLSON

Lord, we thank Thee for that hour
When the stone was rolled away.
Sin and death had lost their power,
Earth could sing that Easter Day—
Sing of Thy redemptive dying
And the sacrifice it meant,
Of man's debt the rectifying,
And Thy grace from heaven sent.

Lord, we thank Thee that our groping
Through the centuries was done,
Pardon for which we were hoping
Had by Thee been amply won.
May we cease our futile striving,
Claim the grace that will suffice,
Dedicate to Thee our living,
Knowing Thou hast paid the price.

147

And He departed from our sight that we might return to our heart, and there find Him.

—SAINT AUGUSTINE

*Sunset at Cape Kiwanda, Oregon.
Photograph © Dennis Frates*

THE RESURRECTION
OF DREAMS

PAMELA KENNEDY

I have always been a planner. As a child I organized my dolls and planned their daily activities. In school I thrived in a classroom with an organized teacher and felt adrift when assigned to a less-structured, spontaneous sort. Lists and schedules became my security—a way to control and direct the uncertainties of life, a way to realize my dreams.

As a young wife I took pride in maintaining an orderly home. Grocery shopping was done on a budget and with a list. Housework was organized by each day. Work came before play and duty before relaxation. With an orderly approach, life was manageable. I knew my dreams could be achieved with the appropriate amount of organization and hard work.

And then we decided to have a family. According to my timeline, it was time to begin to have babies one year after marriage. One year passed, then two, then three, and no babies arrived. The structure of my life started to crumble. Frantic to regain control, I became more organized—reading, studying, seeking guidance from experts in infertility.

Three years turned to five, and still no babies came. Slowly I began to accept the death of my dream—my dream of a house full of laughing children, of walks in the park and noisy family holidays. Year by year, tear by tear, the dream faded. It could not be bought with all the power of my will, nor all the planning of my heart.

Then a new hope flickered. We began to explore adoption. But circumstances conspired against us: there were few babies available, the waiting time was more than two years, and my husband was due to be transferred within eighteen months. Appointments with social workers were delayed or canceled.

Then the impossible happened. On a sunny June day, four weeks before we were to move, we walked out of the adoption center carrying our seven-week-old son. No amount of planning, preparing, or maneuvering had brought about this miracle. It

Photograph © Christoph Becker/Minden Pictures

was simply an act of God's mercy. It was the resurrection of hope from a dead dream.

So often we experience the loss of hope when our dreams die. Perhaps a relationship fails, a promise is broken, a child disappoints. We plunge into the tomb-like darkness of despair, certain that life will never be bright again. It is at this point, however, that God often works His greatest miracle. It is the miracle of the Resurrection. He is not limited by the death of our dreams but enabled by it. For when our hands are emptied of our own plans, He is able to fill them with His abundance.

That first Easter morning, Mary, Peter, John, and the others believed their dreams were dead, trapped in a stony crypt. What God revealed, however, was a new dream far more wonderful than they could have imagined. Where they saw death, He had prepared new life and a dream that changed the course of history.

When you believe your dreams have died, look upon the empty tomb. In His loving mercy, God has a new dream waiting for you, a lively hope made possible because of the Resurrection of His Son.

LOVEST THOU ME?

PETER MARSHALL

O*nce again the disciples* were gathered together, Thomas among them. Suddenly Jesus was with them in the room. He singled Thomas out, smiled at him: "Reach hither thy finger, and behold my hands; and reach hither thy hand, and thrust it into my side; and be not faithless, but believing."

Thomas was all but overwhelmed. Gone was all his blustering skepticism. He fell to his knees . . . All he could say was "My Lord and my God."

Simon Peter witnessed this. There was now no doubt in his heart . . . something tremendous had indeed happened. The Christ who had been crucified was alive . . . Life could never be the same again!

Yet something else troubled Simon, ate at him. He was still nursing deep and bitter shame, still smarting with the searing iron that had eaten into his very soul.

He had denied his Lord. How could he ever face Him again?

Whenever Simon was deeply troubled, always he went back to his nets. "I go a-fishing," he would say. And this time, six of his friends decided to go with him.

There came the night when the men had worked hard and had caught nothing. As they rowed back towards shore, discouraged and in comparative silence, they saw someone standing on the beach in the early light of morning. The sea was calm—calm as a millpond—and a light early-morning mist still clung to the surface of the water.

"Children, have ye any meat?"

And when they replied in the negative, the voice called: "Cast the net on the right side of the ship, and ye shall find."

They had nothing to lose in following the stranger's advice. Over the side went the nets again, this time with success—so much success that the nets were in danger of breaking.

They were now getting closer to the shore, and the mist was beginning to lift. They could see flames leaping from a fire on the beach, and this mysterious figure

150

Hasley Basin in White River National Forest, Colorado. Photograph © Carr Clifton

waiting for them to beach their boat. "It is the Lord," said John, and that was enough for Simon. Here was the opportunity for which he had longed—to tell the Lord that he loved Him—to show how well he knew Him. Without a moment's hesitation, he jumped overboard and waded ashore.

And then comes the loveliest record of God dealing with a penitent sinner. . . . Its tenderness and understanding come stealing into our own hearts like the perfume of crushed flowers. As they sat round the fire, cooking some of the fish they had caught and baking their loaves of bread on the live coals, Jesus suddenly turned to Simon.

"Simon, son of Jonas, lovest thou me more than these?"

Simon was a little puzzled at the question: "Yes, Lord, Thou knowest that I love Thee."

Christ looked him straight in the eyes. "Then—feed my sheep."

But when the question came a second, and then a third time, light began to dawn for Simon. For every one of Simon's earlier denials, Jesus was now asking a pledge of love. This was His way of making everything all right again. When next we see Simon, he is Simon no more—but Peter—the Rock. We see him fearless and eloquent, fire in his eyes and his voice vibrant with conviction, melodious with good news. His own will has gone; his Master's will has taken its place. Peter stands up and preaches the Gospel of his crucified and risen

Lord. Furthermore, he is preaching it in Jerusalem, at the storm-center of the enemies of the Nazarene.

Implicit in the whole situation is the fact that, on the day of the Crucifixion, the disciples did not ever expect to see Christ again. The Resurrection was the last thing they expected. Their belief in it was not some fantastic idea, wafted in from the swamps of fevered imaginations. It was not some romantic wish out of their dream-house, not the result of wishful thinking. For it had come as a complete shock, unexpected, bewildering.

There is no more adamant fact in the records than the changes that came over these men. Jerusalem had been anything but impressed with the way Christ's disciples had conducted themselves during the arrest and trial of the Nazarene.

His followers had certainly not been courageous. In fact, they had all either fled to save their own lives or followed at a great distance. Peter was so fearful that he had even denied having known the Nazarene. Then, after their Master's death, the band of disciples had stayed in hiding with the doors locked—"for fear of the Jews."

Yet after that first Easter morning, we find these same men—timid, frightened, ineffective—preaching openly, with no fear of anyone.

Their personal conviction rings like a bell through the pages of the New Testament . . . steady and strong . . . "That which we have heard with our own ears, seen with our own eyes, handled with our own hands, declare we unto you."

And of what were they so sure? That Jesus Christ was alive—but no spiritual resurrection this—not just the perpetuation of a dead man's ideas.

No, by a Resurrection they meant that on a certain Sabbath, suddenly, at a given time between sunset and dawn, in that new tomb which had belonged to Joseph of Arimathea, there had been a fluttering of unseen forces . . . a rustling as of the breath of God moving through the garden. Strong, immeasurable life had been breathed back into the dead body they had laid upon the cold stone slab. And the dead man had risen up, had come out of the grave-clothes, had walked to the threshold of the tomb, had stood swaying for a moment on His wounded feet, and had walked out into the dewy garden alive forevermore.

It was so real to them that they could have almost heard the whispered sigh as the spirit had fluttered back into the worn body, almost caught a whiff of the strange scents that had drifted back to Him from he tomb of linen and bandages . . . of spices—myrrh and aloes . . . and close air and blood.

Furthermore, they were saying these things in the same city that had sought to destroy the Christ, right at the door of the stronghold of the priests, a thousand paces from the tomb where Christ had been laid.

Christ's enemies would have given anything to have refuted their claims. One thing would have done it—so simply. If only they could have produced a body. But they could not. . . .

No tabloid will ever print the startling news that the mummified body of Jesus of Nazareth has been discovered in old Jerusalem. Christians have no carefully embalmed body enclosed in a glass case to worship. Thank God, we have an empty tomb.

The glorious fact that the empty tomb proclaims to us is that life for us does not stop when death comes. Death is not a wall, but a door. And eternal life, which may be ours now, by faith in Christ, is not interrupted when the soul leaves the body, for we live on . . . and on.

There is no death to those who have entered into fellowship with Him who emerged from the tomb. Because the Resurrection is true, it is the most significant thing in our world today. Bringing the Resurrected Christ into our lives, individual and national, is the only hope we have for making a better world. "Because I live, ye shall live also."

That is the message of Easter.

153

FEED MY SHEEP

After these things Jesus shewed himself again to the disciples at the sea of Tiberias; and on this wise shewed he himself.

There were together Simon Peter, and Thomas called Didymus, and Nathanael of Cana in Galilee, and the sons of Zebedee, and two other of his disciples.

Simon Peter saith unto them, I go a fishing. They say unto him, We also go with thee. They went forth, and entered into a ship immediately; and that night they caught nothing.

But when the morning was now come, Jesus stood on the shore: but the disciples knew not that it was Jesus. Then Jesus saith unto them, Children, have ye any meat? They answered him, No.

And he said unto them, Cast the net on the right side of the ship, and ye shall find. They cast therefore, and now they were not able to draw it for the multitude of fishes.

Therefore that disciple whom Jesus loved saith unto Peter, It is the Lord. Now when Simon Peter heard that it was the Lord, he girt his fisher's coat unto him, (for he was naked,) and did cast himself into the sea. And the other disciples came in a little ship; (for they were not far from land, but as it were two hundred cubits,) dragging the net with fishes. As soon

then as they were come to land, they saw a fire of coals there, and fish laid thereon, and bread.

Jesus saith unto them, Bring of the fish which ye have now caught.

Simon Peter went up, and drew the net to land full of great fishes, an hundred and fifty and three: and for all there were so many, yet was not the net broken.

Jesus saith unto them, Come and dine. And none of the disciples durst ask him, Who art thou? knowing that it was the Lord.

Jesus then cometh, and taketh bread, and giveth them, and fish likewise.

This is now the third time that Jesus shewed himself to his disciples, after that he was risen from the dead.

So when they had dined, Jesus saith to Simon Peter, Simon, son of Jonas, lovest thou me more than these? He saith unto him, Yea, Lord; thou knowest that I love thee. He saith unto him, Feed my lambs.

He saith to him again the second time, Simon, son of Jonas, lovest thou me? He saith unto him, Yea, Lord; thou knowest that I love thee. He saith unto him, Feed my sheep.

He saith unto him the third time, Simon, son of Jonas, lovest thou me? Peter was grieved because he said unto him the third time,

CHRIST APPEARING TO THE APOSTLES ON THE LAKE OF TIBERIAS, *from the upper section of the Maesta altarpiece, by Duccio di Buoninsegna. Image © Scala/Art Resource, NY*

Lovest thou me? And he said unto him, Lord, thou knowest all things; thou knowest that I love thee. Jesus saith unto him, Feed my sheep.

Verily, verily, I say unto thee, When thou wast young, thou girdest thyself, and walkedst whither thou wouldest: but when thou shalt be old, thou shalt stretch forth thy hands, and another shall gird thee, and carry thee whither thou wouldest not.

This spake he, signifying by what death he should glorify God. And when he had spoken this, he saith unto him, Follow me.

Then Peter, turning about, seeth the disciple whom Jesus loved following; which also leaned on his breast at supper, and said, Lord, which is he that betrayeth thee?

Peter seeing him saith to Jesus, Lord, and what shall this man do?

Jesus saith unto him, If I will that he tarry till I come, what is that to thee? follow thou me.

Then went this saying abroad among the brethren, that that disciple should not die: yet Jesus said not unto him, He shall not die; but, If I will that he tarry till I come, what is that to thee?

This is the disciple which testifieth of these things, and wrote these things: and we know that his testimony is true. And there are also many other things which Jesus did, the which, if they should be written every one, I suppose that even the world itself could not contain the books that should be written. Amen.

Easter Morning

EDMUND SPENSER

Most glorious Lord of life, that on this day
Didst make Thy triumph over death and sin,
And having harrowed hell, didst bring away
Captivity thence captive, us to win;
This joyous day, dear Lord, with joy begin,
And grant that we for whom Thou didst die,
Being with Thy dear blood clean washed from sin,
May live forever in felicity:
And that Thy love we weighing worthily,
May likewise love Thee for the same again:
And for Thy sake, that all like dear didst buy,
With love may one another entertain.
So let us love, dear love, like as we ought;
Love is the lesson which our Lord has taught.

157

*For hope is born
when lilacs bloom
rain-sweet in early
spring, and faith that
found an empty tomb
can conquer anything!*

—HELEN WELSHIMER

Photograph © William H. Johnson

AFTER EASTER, WHAT?

CAROL BESSENT HAYMAN

We have just experienced the self-examination and soul-searching of Lent followed by the Easter experience: the fellowship and confession of the Last Supper, the agony of Christ's last hours on the cross, and finally the triumph and joy of the Resurrection. But after Easter, what? We have tried to see our many faults, have remembered the death and passion of our Lord, and have rejoiced to know "The Lord is Risen." Now we must take our faith and our Christian belief that Jesus really does live and reflect it in our lives. No more doubts, no more fears, no more uncertainty. He *lives* and, because He lives, we too shall live. Remember the lovely solo in Handel's "Messiah"—"I Know that My Redeemer Liveth"? There is no room for doubt or hesitation here. "I KNOW." the soloist says it over and over. "I Know." Do *we* know? Christ has said "Go ye into all the world" and "Lo, I am with you always." . . .

Nineteen centuries ago the "faithful eleven" were commissioned to "go and preach." Their response changed the world for all time to come. The power of God was upon them. This was no weeping, discouraged, "sheep-without-a-shepherd" group. Their hearts were on fire with His Gospel, their hands and feet quick to carry His message, their tongues never tired of telling the story of His love; and many willingly died martyrs' deaths because of their total commitment to Christ and the way of life He had taught them.

Today we have the same message, the same promise. What will be our response? Now that the Easter glory is past, what? Will that glory remain in your life and mine? Will it make us better Christians, more willing to love our fellowman and let God's will be done in our lives? There is no other way. Anything less makes Easter just another date on the calendar, instead of the supreme sacrifice of a loving God who made death only a doorway to eternal life and brought hope for a better world to all mankind. Vincent G. Burns has said, "God lives in human hearts—in thine, in mine. We are vessels of a life divine, and every human breast a holy shrine." How about you and me? For us, after Easter, what?

Photograph © Akira Takano/relax/Jupiter Images

Index

160